ENCOUNTERING GOD IN THE MARGINS

Encountering God in the Margins

VERITAS

This edition published 2010 by
Veritas Publications
7–8 Lower Abbey Street
Dublin 1, Ireland
Email publications@veritas.ie
Website www.veritas.ie

ISBN 978 1 84730 220 5
Copyright © Aidan Donaldson, 2010
Scripture taken from The Good News Bible (London: Collins, 1971)

10 9 8 7 6 5 4 3 2 1

A catalogue record for this book is available from the
British Library.
Cover designed by Lir Mac Cárthaigh.

Printed in the Republic of Ireland by ColourBooks Ltd, Dublin

Veritas books are printed on paper made from the wood pulp
of managed forests. For every tree felled, at least one tree is
planted, thereby renewing natural resources.

To my dear wife, Philomena,
my three lovely daughters,
Caoimhe, Eadaoin and Grainne,
my son-in-law, Ian,
and my loving parents,
Joe and Alice Donaldson.

To Catholic missionaries,
lay and religious, throughout
the world and to all other
justice volunteers who act in the
spirit of solidarity, which leads
them to the margins.

To all who are oppressed by
poverty and injustice.

ACKNOWLEDGEMENTS

Without the support of my family and friends I would not have been able to take even the first steps on this journey. To them and all people of good will who have encouraged and supported me in my immersion journey into the margins, I am deeply grateful.

The opportunity to go to the margins could only have come about with the prompting and guidance of many within the Blessed Edmund Rice Network. In particular, I am indebted to Tony Twomey, Donal Leader, Fergus Reilly, Seamus O'Reilly and Tom Kearney – all members of the Christian Brothers.

To the Board of Governors of St Mary's CBGS, its teachers and all members of staff, students and parents, I offer my sincerest gratitude. In particular, I would like to thank my former principal, Kevin Burke, my current principal, Jim Sheerin, and my colleagues, Br James McKenna and Mark Robinson, for their most generous understanding, support and friendship.

Special thanks to Br John McCourt, Fr Edgar Pillet, Angela Miyanda, Peter Tembo, Br Jacek, Fr Oswald Mallya, Cecilia Nyasulu, Yvonne Bwala, Derek Himwaze and Osten Mukonka. This story would not have been possible without my encounters with these modern-day prophets.

A very special mention must be given to Fr Peter McVerry, who guided, encouraged, challenged and advised me throughout the writing of this book.

Thanks also to Catherine Gough, Donna Doherty and Amanda Conlon-McKenna of Veritas Publications who, through their patience and expertise, have made this book a much more finished work.

Final acknowledgement and thanks to all of the Project Zambia volunteers and supporters and to the people of Kabwata, Misisi, Mapepe and Kibera. This is your story. God bless you all.

CONTENTS

Becoming Fully Immersed: Experiences in Mapepe

Foreword – Peter McVerry SJ

'I WAS SEVENTEEN years old when I first went into a leper hospital and held in my arms a man with leprosy. He wept ... so did I.' So said John Allen, a final-year student in Drogheda CBS who had been on an immersion experience in India. This young man is unlikely to ever forget this moment; it was potentially a life-changing experience, a religious conversion.

When God became a human being, God did not come as a powerful king who could command allegiance, nor as a respected religious leader who could inspire millions to follow him. Instead, God became a suffering victim of religious and political oppression. In that human being, hanging on the cross, unjustly condemned to death, God was to be found.

This book is about finding God. It reminds us that we cannot find God in our churches, in our tabernacles, unless we first find God in those human beings who are suffering and marginalised by the political, economic, social and sometimes religious oppression of today. It reminds us that we cannot worship God with hymns and incense unless we first worship God in the broken bodies of those whom society ignores. It is a modern-day re-telling of the words of the prophet Isaiah, unheeded in our time as in his:

> What are your endless sacrifices to me? Says Yahweh,
> I am sick of holocausts of rams and the fat of calves ...
> Bring me your worthless offerings no more ...
> You may multiply your prayers, I shall not listen ...
> (Isaiah 1:11-15)

> Is not this the sort of fast that pleases me
> To break unjust fetters
> And undo the thongs of the yoke.
> To let the oppressed go free
> And break every yoke,
> To share your bread with the hungry,
> And shelter the homeless poor.
>
> (Isaiah 58:6-7)

The supreme act of obedience by Jesus to his Father was his total self-giving on the Cross for the sake of his brothers and sisters. This book challenges the followers of Jesus to ask: 'Why, when the Christian community, in millions of Churches around the world, at every moment of every day of every year, remembers, re-enacts, in its Eucharistic celebration, this act of total self-giving by its leader, Jesus, does the exploitation, suffering and exclusion of millions of human beings in our world, and in each of our nations and communities, continue to exist?'

God is surely outraged at the unnecessary suffering inflicted on so many of God's own beloved children, suffering caused by the greed and abuse of power by others. But if God is outraged, we, the disciples, have lost our sense of outrage. The destitution of many in far off countries, the homelessness of many at home, the exploitation of people and their resources for the benefit of a privileged few, the death of countless children from starvation and easily preventable disease, the use of children as labourers or sex workers and the political and economic structures that condemn those people to poverty, marginalisation and early death no longer outrage us. We have lost our sense of outrage because we have lost our sense of God. The biblical God of liberation and fulfilment, revealed in Jesus Christ, has been replaced by a God of the Temple, to be worshipped with songs of praise in the quiet and comfort of our hallowed Churches, without having to be worried about what is happening in the world outside the walls. Jesus himself has become someone to be adored in the tabernacle, rather than someone to be followed and imitated in his self-giving. The God who spoke through the prophets, challenging, making people and rulers uncomfortable and demanding justice, has been silenced in our time.

I doubt that anyone reading this book can be unmoved at the stories of poverty and suffering they tell. What screams from these pages is the unfairness of it all. We cannot avoid comparing the life we live, with its superfluities and comforts, with the lives of many others who live in poverty, often on the edge of destitution. Life for them need not be like this, should not be like this. This book tells stories of people who have given their lives and sacrificed their comforts to make life for others a little more endurable. They have heard 'the cry of the poor', a cry which calls for action, which demands a response. Those who have responded do not complain about the inaction of the rest of us or of political leaders; they are simply so busy, so absorbed in the work that they do that they have no time to whinge. But they have every right to do so, because we have failed, not just them, but those they serve.

This book is about the experience of immersion, that leap of faith into the dark which brings people into the communities and lives of others living on the edge. The motivations for taking such a jump into the unknown may have been unclear and varied. Some may have gone to have a good time, others may have thought they were going to save the world, but few came back unchanged. They went to give, and they did indeed give something, but they received far more than they could ever give. Those living in poverty and in the margins had something to give them that MasterCard could never buy. Like that man hanging on the cross, ignored, laughed at, despised by all who passed by, they revealed the face of God to those who had eyes to see.

The immersion experience is not one for those who are attached to their comforts – physical or psychological. It challenges our lifestyle, it questions us on the meaning of our lives, and it can, if we let it, draw out of us everything that is best in a human being, a spirit of self-sacrifice that our sense of solidarity with the oppressed and exploited requires from us. We become, then, a true follower of that man hanging on the cross.

Fr Peter McVerry SJ

Preface

> Through love we can open ourselves in such a way
> to God and others that we completely empty
> ourselves and fill ourselves in the same proportion
> with the reality of others and God. It is precisely this
> that occurred in the case of Jesus Christ. In other
> human beings, sisters and brothers of Jesus, we have
> received from God and Jesus the same challenge: to
> open ourselves more and more to everything and to
> everybody so that we can be the fullness of divine
> and human communication like Christ.[1]

Approximately a decade ago, the Christian Brothers'
Leadership Team in Ireland invited its schools to participate
in a new initiative called the Developing World Immersion
Programme. This initially involved senior school students
and members of staff trying to establish bonds of fraternal
solidarity and mutual love with some of those for whom life
is a struggle against poverty, injustice and oppression. In
many ways, the immersion programme is an invitation to go
to the missions and become disciple. Over the past years,
many within the Edmund Rice Network have been going off
to work with and be with some of the poorest and most
marginalised communities in Latin America, India and
Africa. I started my African journey some seven years ago as
part of our school's (St Mary's Christian Brothers' Grammar
School) response to the invitation to 'go to the margins and
become immersed'. It was only in the slums of Lusaka and
the surrounding villages in Zambia that I came to
understand what 'being immersed' truly means. 'Immersion'

does not mean being a visitor or dropping into a community to engage in some sort of charity work or 'volunteer tourism', which has become so fashionable in the West today. Immersion is about justice, it is about standing in radical solidarity with the dispossessed, marginalised and ignored communities who are kept in crushing poverty by a global economic and political system so that some – especially us in the affluent Western world – can live in opulence. Immersion is about becoming an advocate on behalf of these victims of injustice. It is about being the voice of the voiceless. It is about coming to know the names of the marginalised so that you can truly become their voice, just as they have become our voice of introduction to their communities in the so-called Developing World. Immersion is about leaving your comfort zone, unplugging yourself from the matrix and seeing the world the way it truly is, not just the world of consumerism filtered through to us by a dehumanising, stultified diet of the mass media, advertising and reality television.

The comfort zone I left was Belfast. As a teacher of Religious Education at St Mary's CBGS, I was always intrigued by the unconditional response of the early disciples to the invitation by the young rabbi walking by the Sea of Galilee to 'come, follow me'. When the invitation to go to witness the missions for myself was extended to me by my then principal, Kevin Burke, I did not jump at it with the enthusiasm of the Galilean fishermen or of Matthew the tax collector. A mixture of cynicism, a (natural) reluctance to leave my comfort zone and uncertainty and fear did not make me an ideal early recruit. Yet, with prompting from Kevin and after listening to stories from others who had been on immersion, I found myself boarding a plane to Lusaka, into the yet-to-be discovered world of immersion. The slums and townships of Misisi, Kamwala and Kabwata, as well as the villages of Old Kabweza and Mapepe, now feel like places of belonging and, paradoxically, places of hope, friendship and, above all else, love. The immersion programme that began at St Mary's has now grown to become a much larger justice organisation involving parishes, community groups, other schools and many individuals from wide and diverse backgrounds, including different social, religious, cultural and spiritual outlooks: Project Zambia. In the same vision and energy of the Christian Brothers' Developing World Immersion Programme, Project Zambia goes to the above named and other communities to become part of a living movement of mutual affirmation, a celebration of our common humanity and God-given dignity. It is a witness against a world order that celebrates greed over sharing, profit over need, materialism over spirituality, individualism over community, destruction over care, death over life and injustice over justice. In short, immersion is about revolution. It is about placing people and love and justice and freedom at the centre of the world and standing with those who have been made victims of injustice, poverty, oppression and neglect by the powerful, the rich and those who simply do not care.

For many people, Africa can appear to be a place without hope of transformation or improvement, never mind salvation. Despite the enormous sums of aid and charity directed at the Third World in general and Africa in particular, it seems that nothing changes. The standard Western view of African society is that endemic and systematic corruption, along with incompetence and a serious lack of work ethic, has self-condemned Africa to the dreadful state that persists there. For some, Zambia may well be a case in point. A huge country (almost ten times the size of Ireland) with an exceptionally young population (in a total of approximately eleven million people) and blessed with a climate, soil and rivers that could provide as much maize as could feed all of southern Africa. Yet, instead of being self-sufficient, or even wealthy, Zambia is one of the poorest countries in the world today … and it is getting poorer. According to the UNHCR, the average life expectancy in Zambia in 2004 was 32.4 years.[2] This is almost twenty years less than the average life expectancy in Zambia some four decades ago, as is the case with every country in sub-Saharan Africa. Given that the HIV/AIDS pandemic is still rising in Zambia, this figure of life expectancy will continue to drop, as will the number of orphans rise. Currently, almost one million children in Zambia are orphans. When the grandparent carers die – many of whom we work along with in Mapepe and Misisi – another issue will have to be faced: orphan-led households. If this is not bad enough, 80 per cent of Zambians are living on one US dollar a day.

It is little wonder that some of us in the affluent world go into a 'can't do anything so don't care' mode. Others of us go into 'charity' mode – Africa is a sick child and a problem that needs our help and support. Both attitudes are equally wrong and fatally flawed. The former, to do nothing, is a natural surrender and acquiescence to the individualism and egoism of the consumerist world of affluence that characterises and defines much of the West. The latter suggests that Africa is a 'self-made problem' or 'natural disaster' that needs to be fixed by the West. Nothing could be further from the truth. The crushing poverty and its consequences for the people of Africa is neither natural nor self-made. Poverty in the Third World is a crime deliberately committed by and sustained by the economic and political system that dominates all of our lives, whether we live in materially rich Western societies or in the impoverished margins where the vast majority of the population seek to survive. The poor and oppressed of Africa – and the other communities who live in the margins, be they in Latin America, Asia or in our own marginalised and invisible communities in Ireland and other countries in the so-called Developed World – need justice, not charity.

I have been truly blessed in my time on immersion to meet and be touched by some of the most inspirational people God, in his infinite wisdom, could ever have placed me with. This book is simply a collection of true stories, reflections, responses and dialogues, which are a result of one immersion volunteer's experiences in Africa. The names of the places and of the individuals may seem strange or unfamiliar to the reader at first; they were to me also. I have come to know, embrace and love all of these people and spaces. They have become family to me, just as the places have now taken on a sense of closeness, of identity, of being at home with oneself and others – what Germans call 'Heimat' – a sense of perhaps what Jesus encouraged us to build throughout his teachings and through his actions: the Kingdom of God. Immersion has given this pilgrim an opportunity to encounter many remarkable people and experience emotions and face challenges of a unique nature. For that I am truly grateful.

Introduction:

Our Topsy-Turvy World

The world we live in is a very strange place indeed. It is, in fact, an upside down world that needs to be revolved. The world needs a revolution – and so do we. However, before the reader panics, becomes fearful, dismissive or just bored and thinks that he/she is about to enter the clichéd and infantile considerations of a social revolutionary harking back to an imagined revolutionary era, please give me a little time to explain my case. The world we live in is indeed a peculiar, contradictory and confusing place: fabulously rich yet incredibly poor; technologically advanced and knowledgeable on the one hand, yet committing environmental suicide on the other; able to transport millions of holiday-makers to far-off destinations and hedonistic 'paradises' every day, while unable (read 'unwilling') to send some of the surplus food in the affluent Western world to feed those who are starving in the Developing World. By the way, if you need to impose a war on people in some far off country, don't panic. It seems that in today's world there is no shortage of materials to use in conflict. After all, the arms industry is the single biggest industry in the world with over a trillion US dollars being spent on weapons annually. We may not be surprised at this, but we should be shocked, disgusted and angered. Former US president, Dwight D. Eisenhower, pointed out the real effects the arms trade has on humanity when he stated the following in a speech on 16 April 1953:

Every gun that is made, every warship launched, every rocket fired signifies, in the final sense, a theft from those who hunger and are not fed, those who are cold and are not clothed. The world in arms is not spending money alone. It is spending the sweat of its laborers, the genius of its scientists, and the hopes of its children ... This is not a way of life at all, in any true sense. Under the cloud of threatening war, it is humanity hanging from a cross of iron.[3]

Modern society does not have any difficulty in finding that other crucial commodity for making war: disposable humans and other victims without whom such lucrative activity could not take place. Nor does modern society have moral qualms when it comes to dealing with the rather awkward issue of civilian deaths, simply reclassifying such killings as 'collateral damage'.

This term of military doublespeak, which is defined by the USAF Intelligence Targeting Guide as '[the] unintentional damage or incidental damage affecting facilities, equipment, or personnel, occurring as a result of military actions directed against targeted enemy forces or facilities. Such damage can occur to friendly, neutral, and even enemy forces',[4] first emerged in the Vietnam War and has subsequently become almost an accepted description in (at least) much of the US media when describing the killing of men, women and children in the Iraq and Afghan conflicts. The United States Department of Defense has given a very clear codified version of what is a chilling demonstration of how such language negates the human dignity of those who are on the receiving end of 'collateral damage'. According to

Joint Publication 3-16, collateral damage is '[the] unintentional or incidental injury or damage to persons or objects that would not be lawful military targets in the circumstances ruling at the time. Such damage is not unlawful so long as it is not excessive in light of the overall military advantage anticipated from the attack'. Nor is such a term unique in the vocabulary of the powerful who seek to deny recognition of basic humanity to the powerless. Those countries in abject poverty are referred to as 'the *Developing* World' as if they are progressing or moving forward in some way, whereas clearly they are being moved precisely in the opposite direction! Globalisation – one of the major causes of poverty – is presented as a *solution* to the problems of the poverty-stricken countries. Structural adjustment mechanisms and other so-called developmental policies are put into place by rich governments to enslave and ensnare the poor countries even more. It is little wonder that we need to stand the world the right way up.

Where does immersion come into all of this? Quite simply, to become immersed is to say 'no' to the way the world is and begin to create a new world built not on injustice, greed, individualism and passivity, but rather a world based on justice, community, solidarity, action and love of the other. In short, immersion is to help the world stand the correct way up. To allow oneself to become immersed in the margins is to abandon and reject the power structures and social practices that keep the Third World poor and oppressed, and to become part of something much bigger, infinitely more intelligent and rational, and certainly more real, necessary and true than anything the false world we live in can ever offer. Immersion is nothing less than building the Kingdom of God.

Entering into Immersion

Chapter 1

An Invitation to Immersion

ON 21 DECEMBER 2001, I popped into the office of Kevin Burke, the principal of St Mary's Christian Brothers' Grammar School. It was the last day of term and the staff were getting ready to go out for Christmas lunch. I knew that Kevin had wanted to have a word with me – something about some new Christian Brothers' initiative, apparently. As the school co-ordinator of Edmund Rice activities, I had worked closely with Kevin and many others throughout the school community and the Edmund Rice Network in promoting the vision of Blessed Edmund and the radical social practice that emanates from it. I wondered what the latest venture would be. A youth conference? Perhaps some local outreach programme? Maybe a new journal or other publication to be disseminated throughout the school? However, it was nothing quite as normal or straightforward as that. He suggested that I might go to Africa.

'Kevin, it is a total waste of money and time and I am not going. Our school should not touch this nonsense with a forty-foot barge pole!' I was reacting to Kevin's suggestion that our school should become involved with the Christian Brothers' immersion programme. I had heard of this programme from the involvement of another local Christian Brothers' school (Glen Road Christian Brothers' College), which had sent a group of students and staff to India a year previous. The thinking behind the immersion programme is that by encouraging people from affluent parts of the world to go to the undeveloped world and 'immerse' themselves with communities there, participants will develop bonds of mutual friendship, partnership and solidarity with the host communities, as well as come to a deeper understanding of the causes and effects of poverty and injustice. I was entirely sceptical of such ventures. For me, and many others I am sure, the idea of a bunch of people, many with no particularly relevant contributory skills, travelling from Ireland to an impoverished community somewhere in the Third World smacked of poverty tourism and misguided goodwill, with a touch of paternalistic arrogance and voyeurism. Not only that, it also struck me as a distinct waste of valuable money, which could be spent on helping people rather than on airfares and other expenses. 'If a school wants to help poor people in the Third World, they should raise a lot of money and send it all out to the people there', was my considered reaction.

Kevin noted my concerns and went on to explain that the Christian Brothers felt that it was important for our schools to go to the margins, to demonstrate solidarity with the poor and oppressed, to show the people there that they have not been abandoned and forgotten but that they are valued, to witness to the Gospel and to make a difference. Kevin went on to inform me that it had been proposed to extend the immersion process to include Africa, with

Zambia as a starting point, and that St Mary's CBGS had been selected as one of the first cohort of schools to be invited. He was asking me to go on an inspection trip in the following June on behalf of the school to assess the feasibility and value of such a venture. 'Besides', he said, 'if you find that it is a waste of time, energy or resources then bring that back in your report and we will simply drop the project.'

There was no getting out of it and, anyway, it would take me no time at all to get the conclusive evidence I would need to tell Kevin, the Board of Governors, the Christian Brothers' Leadership Team and anyone else promoting such ventures that, at best, they were misguided or, at worst, it was self-indulgent nonsense which raised false hopes among the host communities and reinforced a patronising attitude and relationship both in Ireland and in Africa. Little did I know just how little I knew!

The next months consisted of an intensive series of meetings, enculturation sessions, medical briefings, injections and all other preparations deemed necessary for people going to Africa for the first time. If one could become an expert on going to the Third World through reading and listening, I was that expert. We were informed that the immersion site for St Mary's CBGS and Monkstown CBS would be Lusaka, the capital of Zambia. Unlike the other schools from Ireland who were going to look at already existent Christian Brothers' mission programmes in places such as Livingstone, Mazabuka, Kabwe, Mongu and Mufulira, we would have to identify immersion programmes in Lusaka ourselves, since the Christian Brothers did not have any schools, orphanages or other projects in Lusaka. Their presence there was very much of an administrative nature. That didn't concern me very much since I was absolutely certain that there were bound to be lots of impoverished communities in Lusaka who (in my Western mentality) spent their entire lives in fervent hope and prayer that salvation might arrive in the guise of some white outsiders to save them. Besides, it would be a waste of time anyway, wouldn't it?

Encountering the fruits of immersion for the first time

The first awareness I experienced that immersion just might not be quite the waste of time that I was sure it would be hit me at a preparation meeting in early 2002 in Dublin. The meeting was a gathering of all those who were going to Zambia that year for their inspection visit and a chance for us to share our hopes, fears, expectations, ideas and so on. The closing session was given by a young man called John Allen, a final year student from Drogheda CBS, who had been on immersion in India the previous year. What could a fresh-faced eighteen-year-old boy tell me about the world, life or anything?

'I was seventeen years old when I first went into a leper hospital and held in my arms a man with leprosy. He wept ... so did I.' The hairs on the back of my neck still stand up when I think of the opening remark from that remarkable young man. He then went on to outline his experiences and how encountering those in the margins changed him, transformed him, energised him. This was not some pious claim from an innocent, naïve youth, rather it was an accurate statement of fact. Within this young man – as well as in his fellow immersion travellers whom we met that day – there was something that was different, new and, above all else, *alive*. Of course they were still ordinary young guys in the sense that they still possessed the normal trappings of modern society – mobile phones, iPods, the normal interests of young people and so on – but the focus or centre of their lives seemed to have had a paradigm shift. 'I now know what is important in life and want to live my life accordingly', was how John Allen put it. And he said it like he meant it.

I pondered on the notion of *metanoia*, that concept of transformation that lies at the heart of much of Christian hope. Coming from the Greek 'μετάνοια' for repentance, *metanoia*, as it is used in the New Testament, has a deeper and more fundamental meaning. It involves not merely regret of past sin but a recognition by man of a darkened vision of his own condition, in which sin, by separating him from God, has reduced him to a divided, autonomous existence, depriving him of both his natural glory and freedom and a desire to be transformed. To repent is to have a change of heart, a spiritual about-face in one's life. Repentance involves both a change of mind and a change of action, a change that occurs in relationship to God. The account in Acts of the Apostles of 'The Coming of the Holy Spirit' can be seen as a clear and dramatic example of precisely such a transformation and conversion:

> When the day of Pentecost came, all the believers were gathered in one place. Suddenly there was a noise from the sky which sounded like a strong wind blowing, and it filled the whole house where they were sitting.

> Then they saw what looked like tongues of fire which
> spread out and touched each person there. They were
> all filled with the Holy Spirit.
>
> (Acts 2:1-13)

Thus, a group of frightened, uncertain and passive individuals became totally transformed, energised and alive and went out to proclaim the Gospel.

There was something in those young men at that meeting which reminded me of that Gospel story. I had just met a group of young men who were prepared to share their story and to speak about their experience of transformation, and decidedly not in the style of evangelical witness. Rather, they did it naturally, as if through their honest account of what they encountered at the margins and who they had become as a result of this experience might be of interest to us: people who were preparing to go to that precious space for the first time. They did not put any special words on it but, reflecting back now, I feel that I was being invited to enter into immersion, to *become* disciple. Could I catch the flame that had so obviously sparked them to become alive, passionate and aware? Did I want it? Could I handle it? The answer awaited me in Zambia.

First immersion experience: the beginning of my education

Armed with every immunisation and injection recommended and with the firm conviction that I was right about the validity or otherwise of immersion, in spite of the doubts that the encounter with John Allen had placed in my mind, I arrived at Lusaka International Airport on a warm morning in the middle of June, along with the other teachers from Ireland, as we set about our respective immersion inspection visits. The first thing that struck me, both in the airport and on the way to the hostel where I would be staying, was that Lusaka did not look like a modern capital city. The crumbling façade of the main arrivals building and the fact that there were only about seven or eight flights per day, as well as the potholes on the main road going into the city, suggested to me that this place had seen 'better days'. On the way into Lusaka, I noticed that rubbish abounded everywhere, that council workers (mostly women) were brushing the ever-present dust off the roads (as the wind kept blowing it back) and that there were people cycling to the markets in the city defying the laws of gravity with enormous loads of charcoal or vegetables impossibly tied to their bikes. One other thing I noticed was that all along the red dusty road into Lusaka there were men running. As an athlete myself (a former marathon runner), I presumed that Zambia was like Kenya, where long-distance running was a way of life … and a way out of poverty. But these guys were different. They were running to somewhere, with purpose … in suits! I asked Br John McCourt (a Christian Brother of many years in Africa who had picked us up at the airport) what they were doing. 'Trying to get work', was his reply. 'Elaborate', I thought. And he did. 'You see, Aidan, there is practically no permanent paid work for the vast majority of the population in Zambia, so these men have to set off from their homes before dawn to try to get their daily bread. They cannot afford the minibus to Lusaka so they have to run and hope that they can get work in Lusaka. They will have to do the same thing tomorrow and the next day. If they fail then their families do not eat.' I watched as men in their best (only decent) clothes ran alongside us – trying, sweating and smiling. I thought of the line in the Lord's Prayer, 'give us this day our daily bread'.

After a day's orientation in Lusaka, the group split up with most of the other teachers heading off to familiarise themselves with their immersion sites in various parts of the country. My immersion colleagues and I left to try to identify potential immersion projects in and around Lusaka. Br John McCourt was our immersion partner, who proved to be invaluable in introducing us to some truly amazing people, whose lives have now indeed become immersed with our own.

The remarkable Angela Miyanda

If anyone epitomises true Christian love or 'agape' – that other-directed selfless giving – then Angela Miyanda is surely that person. The wife of Godfrey Miyanda, the former deputy president of Zambia, leader of the Heritage Party and, in many people's judgement, one of the only non-corrupt, honest politicians in a country where corruption in politics is almost a given, Angela is one of the most unassuming, dignified and inspirational people I have ever had the privilege to meet. She pointedly refuses to use her husband's profile and contacts to support her own work with orphans, HIV/AIDS victims, refugees and other marginalised and poor people. For Angela, the validity and justification of the work she is doing is of its own intrinsic value and should not need to be bolstered in any way by publicity or contacts of a political nature. I must confess that at first this did not make any sense to me. After all, I thought, surely every possible avenue of support should be utilised and exploited in support of the greater good of those whom she was helping. However, what Angela was doing by shunning this type of publicity was affirming the dignity of those who had already been marginalised by society. For Angela, these people were never to be considered as objects of pity to be used as a backdrop or photo opportunity, which could be construed to be of some advantage to any external agenda. These were people who, despite their disadvantage, poverty, marginalisation and oppression, were deserving of dignity, respect, hope, opportunity and love. By reaching out to them in precisely such a fashion, Angela was communicating to them a sense of their own dignity and value.

Angela runs a number of projects including an orphanage in the Kabwata district of Lusaka. There are some seventy-five plus orphans there in what can only be described as an oasis of peace, calm, love and hope in their troubled lives. We have met so many tremendous people there who have truly lifted our souls and who would restore the hope in the triumph of the human spirit over adversity to even the most pessimistic and cynical of persons. She doesn't call it an orphanage; rather, its full and proper title is The Kabwata Transit Centre and Orphanage and was created by Angela in 1998 to provide shelter and care for AIDS orphans in Lusaka. The primary goal of the Centre is to relocate the children with their extended families and communities or to identify foster carers within Zambia in order to give a permanency and future to the children as they move into adulthood. As well as the orphanage, the programme has expanded to include a school, a mobile clinic, a small farm and banana/agricultural project. The Transit Centre has served more than four hundred children and has sixteen members on its staff. Many of the orphans have gone to university and the vast majority have left the Centre with an education, skill and social network that will give these vulnerable and needy young people the chance of a future.

It was at the Centre that I met Jen, a young orphan from Rwanda who had lost (it was believed) every single member of her family in the 1994 genocide. Her physical survival was a miracle, one of those overlooked by the genocidal paramilitary killers of the Interahamwe as it set about its orgy of killing during the one hundred days of slaughter of Tutsis while the world looked on with passivity and disinterest. I often wondered about that other miracle: her emotional and mental survival. After all, here was a young, cheerful, friendly and altogether normal person who had witnessed one of the most horrific periods of darkness of the twentieth century without her faith in humanity being destroyed. She had long ceased to be a dependent in need of support; she was now a principal carer who gave comfort, guidance, help and love to the young orphans at the orphanage. Hatred, revenge, disconsolateness, self-pity and despair were far from Jen's thoughts as she went about her everyday task of making a difference in the lives of vulnerable orphans.

I don't believe in fairy stories, or at least not the sanitised Disney versions of them. I am also pretty agnostic regarding the existence of guardian angels. However, I do believe that special individuals like Angela can make remarkable things come true. As I mentioned above, the facility at Kabwata was not just an orphanage but also a transit centre through which many of the orphans have been re-connected with their extended families. In 2005, through Angela's tireless efforts, it was discovered that Jen had a half-brother who had also survived the slaughter of 1994, due to the fact that he had been out of Rwanda at the time, and was now living in Norway. She has been reunited with him and now resides with his family in Oslo. She has not forgotten her 'second' family in Zambia. Jen spends much of her time visiting the orphanage in Kabwata and working on behalf of the orphans. Sometimes good things do indeed happen to good people, and they are often made possible by remarkable people such as Angela Miyanda.

Chapter 2

Over the Railway Lines to the St Lawrence Centre

AFTER OUR ORIENTATION sessions in Lusaka and making my primary contacts, I thought I was getting a pretty firm handle on the place. Zambia is rated as belonging very definitely to the ten poorest countries in the world (and slipping further down according to every socio-economic indicator). Difficulties include a massive HIV/AIDS crisis, cholera, malaria, tuberculosis and every other Third World disease, as well as the other multiple problems that are a result of poverty. All of this had led to the collapse of the traditional family structure, an explosion of orphans and street children, a breakdown of the socio-economic infrastructure and a deepening of Zambia's debt crisis. Basically, my first few days in Lusaka confirmed everything I had read about the country. Zambia was incredibly poor and needed help – and specifically *my* help, or so I thought. Then Br John McCourt arrived and took me to meet a person who has totally changed my life. 'Aidan, I have been told by Fr Pillet, a French White Father who has been working here for more than ten years, that there is a really interesting project with quite a bit of potential in the southern part of Lusaka that you guys might want to look at. It's called the St Lawrence Centre and it has a school and a home for street children. I've not been there before but I've been told to bring a vehicle with a high clearance. I've taken the community minibus just in case the road is as bad as Fr Pillet says.'

My first experience of a graded road

For us in the West, roads are rather simple and similar constructions: ideally straight, flat and wide, but this is not always so. Even in Ireland today, we still encounter roads that can test our driving skills as we encounter sharp bends, the odd pothole or two and road width that doesn't easily accommodate the wider vehicles increasingly popular today. Improvements in Ireland's road network over the past two decades have been considerable and our expectation is that they are always hard and firm tarmac passages that enable us to get from A to B as quickly as possible. For the uninitiated, roads in the Third World are different from those we experience and expect in the West – very different indeed.

We turned right off the Chilumbula Road, heading from town through the Kamwala district following Fr Pillet's directions for the St Lawrence Centre. The standard of roads in Lusaka, like everywhere else in sub-Saharan Africa, varies enormously and is dependent upon the importance given to them by the authorities. For example, the Great East Road, which leads from the airport to the centre of Lusaka, is of a very high quality. This is because many prospective business people, foreign dignities, politicians and other 'important' people will travel this road to and from the airport. Other main arterial routes, such as the Great North Road, Kafue Road, Burmah Road and Chilumbula Road, are also of a relatively high standard as they are used to convey goods and bring the most important commodity of all, the extremely cheap labour force (the people from the outlying townships, shanty towns, squatter camps, compounds, slums and villages), into town. It is only when you turn off any of these main roads that you realise all is not well with the Zambian road network and that, in the words of Br John McCourt, 'the transportation infrastructure is creaking under pressure due to a lack of maintenance'.

On this road to the St Lawrence Centre, we were bouncing up and down, even though John had reduced the speed of the minibus to little more than a walking pace. Red dust was flying everywhere, potholes to be avoided, six-foot deep storm drains menacingly inches away at the side of the road and a constant flood of people on their way to work, school, markets and every other aspect of African life to be negotiated through and around. 'This is unbelievable, John', I said as my back took another hit from a pothole Br John had failed to miss. 'This is a graded road, Aidan.[5] It will get worse', John replied, only half-laughing. And he was right. We crossed the railway tracks and entered a new world indeed. The railway tracks mark a separation between some of the less-disadvantaged shanty towns of Lusaka and the absolute extreme poverty of the Misisi slum.[6] It is a sort of no man's land between the almost totally marginalised communities of the Kambata and Kamwala districts and the absolutely marginalised and abandoned people of Misisi.

At the railway tracks: a silent people

At the railway crossing, John carefully positioned the minibus at what seemed an impossible upward angle to ensure that we scraped our way over the tracks. Despite the high wheel clearance, the exposed stones and metal railway lines almost seemed to come through the floor of the minibus as we struggled up and over the railway tracks. Not that there was much chance of us getting hit by a speeding train if we did get stuck on the tracks. With (on a busy day) only two trains coming down this railway – the daily passenger train from Livingstone (which can be a day late in any case) and a cargo train from Dar el Salaam lumbering its way from Tanzania to South Africa via Zimbabwe – the odds of survival were in our favour. It was fascinating to observe the children arranging small stones on top of the rim of the track and see others racing along and chugging like a train as they knocked the stones off at great speed to the whoops and delight of their peers. A couple of years later I observed this happening for real as I sat for several hours at the side of the railway tracks with some of the children waiting for a train to come along and smash their carefully placed stones. What an ambush and what joy!

Something caught my eye as the minibus inched over the railway tracks, which seemed to be intent on taking off as much of the undercarriage as possible. In front of us, on both sides of the dust road, lines of people were sitting – mostly elderly women. Around them were small pyramids of stones, each about one metre high. Some piles contained larger stones, about five centimetres by two centimetres, others were made up of smaller stones of about half that size, while other piles were of stones about the size of the tip of one's finger. No laughter could be heard on this side of the railway tracks, just the constant chip, chip, chip of old women with a chisel in one hand and lump hammer in the other, breaking larger pieces of stone into smaller pieces.

'Building materials, Aidan', John said, 'They break the large rocks down to different gauges and hope to sell them.'

Twelve hours a day sitting cross-legged, breaking rocks in the hot sun or pouring rain for a dollar a day. The joints of their wrists, hips and knees were obviously damaged and crying out in pain, if the nerve endings were still functional and sensitive. The skin on their hands like leather; their buttocks and spines victims also of this torturous work. The reasons they do this are obvious and, in fact, running about them as they work: their grandchildren. In Zambia, as in much of the rest of sub-Saharan Africa, it is all too often the grandmothers who are the primary breadwinners and principal carers for the orphans. This is why these women sit working all day for the pittance they are paid in return for possessing such love for their grandchildren. A dollar purchases one meal of maize per day for these children and gives them a chance of survival in an unjust world. Having endured the harshness and poverty of their own early lives, these women are now forced to endure even more in their old age. If ever I felt I was among a people totally abandoned by the world then this surely was it.

Denied any respite from the constant torturous labour in their old age, these people suffer further injustice from the invasion of their privacy by the poverty tourists for whom no worthwhile visit to a slum is complete or worth the ten dollars they pay to a 'guide' for a 'slum safari' without capturing some images of the 'creatures' which inhabit the slums in their native environment and 'natural' poverty. And the real deal is getting a picture of grandmothers breaking rocks, hopefully with a couple of the grandchildren sitting playing in the dirt and squalor. Capturing a piece of these people's souls on camcorder is an especially treasured trophy that can be replayed in the comfort of living rooms in the affluent West, while friends tut-tut and express with equal measure their sorrow for these 'poor unfortunates' and their admiration for their hosts who actually went into one of these slums to take this footage. 'You must have been very brave, darling', may well be the response at many a social evening in the affluent suburbs. It is little wonder that these women are hostile to the presence of tourists and take great exception to people filming them. The women are not proud of their poverty and resent the *bazungu's*[7] attempts to take pictures of them as if they were creatures in a zoo or exhibition. Sometimes the people stop breaking stones for a minute and chase the tourists away.

Chapter 3

Never Judge a Book by its Cover

LOOKS CAN BE deceptive and first impressions are often misleading. The minibus pulled up at the St Lawrence Centre and we jumped out. I looked around and saw a lot of empty scrub land, save an office, a few classrooms, a water pump, a few other bits and pieces of buildings and not much else. 'Is this it?' I thought as I surveyed the bleak landscape with clouds of sand blowing all around us. 'A really interesting project with quite a bit of potential in the southern part of Lusaka' is how Br John had described it. Well, we were in the southern part of Lusaka, but beyond that I didn't see much potential or any interesting project here. How wrong I was. Fr Pillet was there; beside him stood a small and slight African man. 'You are very welcome, John', the priest said in a heavy French accent, belying more than forty years spent in Africa. 'This must be our visitor from Ireland. You too are very welcome.' We exchanged handshakes and pleasantries before Fr Pillet introduced us to his companion. 'This is Peter Tembo, the Coordinator of the St Lawrence Centre. He will take you around, Aidan.' Then Fr Pillet and Br John went off into an office to discuss some business leaving me with my new acquaintance.

Peter Tembo: a modern-day prophet

Peter took me round the St Lawrence Centre while Fr Pillet and Br John were at their meeting. The St Lawrence Centre was a large piece of barren scrubland, about the size of ten football pitches, located between two railway lines. The Catholic Church had acquired the land from the government with a view to developing it for the good of the people of Misisi Compound. What my eyes saw as nothing except dust and stones, Peter saw as buildings and projects that were just not quite there yet. It was the most peculiar of conversations. Peter would take me to one corner of the Centre and point out a barren piece of scrubland where, he assured me, a medical centre would be built some day. Then we would go to another piece of land where, he would inform me, 'a bakery will be built and it will be beside the agricultural project and farm', none of which yet existed of course, but 'this will all happen soon'. His eyes danced when he imagined the future and saw a dream come true, while mine stayed firmly in the present and saw nothing except the dust and scrub land that was the St Lawrence Centre. 'This guy is a hopeless, naïve, utopian dreamer, blind to the realities of the world', I thought. I was firmly rooted in the real world, but who was really hopeless? Who was really naïve? Who was really blind? Surely in the real world there is no place for Utopia?

Jesus and the not so impossible world of utopia

It was the great mediaeval writer, Thomas More, who introduced us to the concept of 'Utopia' almost five hundred years ago in his work, *Utopia* (1516). This work is based on a play on two Greek words *'utopia'* ('no place') and *'eutopia'* ('good place'). According to More, Utopia is:

[N]ot only the best country in the world, but the only one that has any right to call itself a republic ... The Utopian way of life provides ... the happiest basis for a civilised community.[8]

The idea that, somehow, an alternative society – indeed, community – could not only be anticipated but, in fact, brought about, was, for me, absurd, illogical and impossible. It was thinking the unthinkable, especially here in the slums of Lusaka.

His disciples gathered around him, and he began to teach them: 'Happy are those who know they are spiritually poor; the Kingdom of heaven belongs to them! Happy are those who mourn; God will comfort them! Happy are those who are humble; they will receive what God has promised! Happy are those whose greatest desire is to do what God requires; God will satisfy them fully! Happy are those who are merciful to others; God will be merciful to them! Happy are the pure in heart; they will see God! Happy are those who work for peace; God will call them his children! Happy are those who are persecuted because they do what God requires; the Kingdom of heaven belongs to them! Happy are you when people insult you and persecute you and tell all kinds of evil lies against you because you are my followers. Be happy and glad, for a great reward is kept for you in heaven. This is how the prophets who lived before you were persecuted.'

(Matthew 5:1-15)

To many of those listening to Jesus at the Sermon on the Mount, he must have appeared as a most utopian and radical thinker. Here he was, a young fire-brand rabbi, standing on a hillside and addressing the marginalised and oppressed, just outside the Walls of Jerusalem above which the magnificence of the Temple – from which many people would have been excluded due to their lack of wealth and lowly social status – and what message did he give them? That *theirs* is the Kingdom of God, *they* shall be comforted, *they* shall inherit the earth, *they* shall be satisfied, *they* shall be called sons of God and *they* shall see God. If ever there was a world turned upside down then Jesus had just proclaimed it! Jesus sought to announce a kingdom that was not simply to be in another world (like a heaven to be found solely in the afterlife), nor was it to be a territory or a region under the rule of God as aspired to by some of the more radical Jewish sects such as the Essenes and Zealots. For Jesus, the Kingdom of God was to be nothing less than a new order, a total, global and revolutionary transfiguration of everything that the world then, and now, hitherto deemed impossible. It was, and is, a call to total liberation. This new order was announced by Jesus to the disciples of John the Baptist when they asked him, 'Are you the one John said was going to come, or should we expect someone else?' (Matthew 11:3). Jesus' answer was unequivocal and radical in the extreme. 'Go back and tell John what you are hearing and seeing: the blind can see, the lame can walk, those who suffer from dreaded skin diseases are made clean, the deaf hear, the dead are brought back to life, and the Good News is preached to the poor' (Matthew 11:4-5).

Jesus announces a Kingdom of God that is not to be waited for in a utopian future; rather it is the old world transformed into a new one. For Jesus, utopianism is not some illusory or eschatological project to be realised in the future or some undetermined time. It is, in fact, a most concrete and immediate happening that is to be realised in the here and now. It is the primacy of the utopian over the factual – based on faith, hope and anticipation – that releases the potential of the present and realises a world totally reconciled, a world that is the fulfilment of what we can, and are, creating on earth. It is a world created according to the vision of the Sermon on the Mount and one that throws the world based on given structures and accepted relationships into crisis. The Kingdom of God, the manifestation of the sovereignty and lordship of God over this world, so long anticipated by Jews and many Christians alike, is *announced* by Jesus. Furthermore, and just as dramatically, Jesus understands himself as one who is initiating and inaugurating this Kingdom of God and is, according to the liberation theologian Leonardo Boff, best described by a new title: that of 'Liberator'.[9] The transformation envisaged and initiated by Jesus signifies the realisation of the hope of the abolition and annihilation of all alienation and evil, and all that this means for individuals, society and the cosmos.

Finally, the kingdom announced by Jesus was not, nor was ever meant to be, a given, completed or finished reality. It is a process that we are called to help bring about, to create. The miracles of Jesus and his teachings on the kingdom only make sense if we allow ourselves to become agents in the activity of creating such a kingdom based on justice, respect and Christian love and solidarity. The radical social activist and theologian Fr Peter McVerry points out that the story of the Feeding of the Five Thousand in the Gospel of Matthew is a clear indication of how we must act in participating in the new community that Jesus was inaugurating. Matthew describes the event as follows:

> Jesus got out of the boat, and when he saw the large crowd, his heart was filled with pity for them, and he healed those who were ill. That evening his disciples came to him and said, 'It is already very late, and this is a lonely place. Send the people away and let them go to the villages to buy food for themselves.' 'They don't have to leave,' answered Jesus. 'You yourselves give them something to eat!' 'All we have here are five loaves and two fish,' they replied. 'Then bring them here to me,' Jesus said. He ordered the people to sit down on the grass; then he took the five loaves and the two fish, looked up to heaven, and gave thanks to God. He broke the loaves and gave them to the disciples, and the disciples gave them to the people. Everyone ate and had enough. Then the disciples took up twelve baskets full of what was left over. The number of men who ate was about 5,000, not counting the women and children.
>
> (Matthew 14:14-21)

McVerry points out that 'the feeding of the multitudes is understood to be a task for the disciples' and goes on to tell us that 'the disciples feed the poor by sharing what resources they have amongst themselves'.[10] Leaving aside what actually happened at this incident – whether or not Jesus actually transformed the five loaves and two fish into sufficient food for the multitude – what is of crucial significance regarding this episode is that it is illustrative of the Kingdom of God, where the building of this new community rests upon our positive response to the invitation to create this kingdom through reaching out to the poor and marginalised and addressing their needs. Without this dimension, the story of the Feeding of the Five Thousand, like the rest of the miracles, remains a remarkable and seemingly impossible (for humans) action devoid of sacred, salvific meaning.

Hope and Utopia are all around us – if we look

The people who live in the margins feel abandoned precisely because they have been abandoned. Homeless people in Ireland, the travelling community, drug abusers, the unemployed, immigrants and other groups of non-persons in the affluent world, the slum dwellers in the Third World and victims of climate change – all of these people are the victims of a social order that doesn't care about them. They are also necessary victims of an economic order that needs them to be sacrificed so that the rich and powerful can continue to be rich and powerful. It was exactly the same at the time of Jesus. Hence, he proclaimed a kingdom that was based on the very opposite to what our kingdom of affluence is based on: greed, individualism, inequality, exclusion and injustice. The kingdom Jesus outlined in the Sermon of the Mount, and throughout his teachings and affirmed through his actions, is based on real respect for the dignity of others, especially the poor, and a genuine commitment towards ensuring that the needs of all, again, especially the poor, are met even if this means that the material abundance of the West will have to be given up in

45

order to meet the needs of others. If we are sincere about abolishing poverty, we will have to be prepared to abolish our affluent Western lifestyle.

I imagine I would have been like some of the rich people standing on the fringes of the crowd listening with incredulity, and perhaps even anger, at the teacher who was filling heads (and hearts) with such dangerous foolishness. Even if I admired the idealism of the message, I am sure that I would have shaken my head in disbelief and walked away back into the real world, which laughs at such impossible imaginings. I probably felt much the same at this first meeting with Peter Tembo. How could he and his people, who had nothing and were (and still are) nothing in the eyes of those in power, achieve such a transformation of a piece of squalid scrub land? This man, I thought, clearly needs to be educated in the causes of his community's poverty and the solution. This is why I came to Zambia. I was well prepared for this or any other encounter. After all, in the six months I had been given by the Christian Brothers to prepare to go to Zambia, I had read everything about sub-Saharan Africa, the politics and economy of the Third World and Zambia in particular. So, was I not an expert on everything pertaining to that part of the world by now? Therefore, I started to share with Peter some of my 'knowledge' and teach him about the country and community he had lived in all of his life and how to change it. After I had given a semi-lecture on debt relief, international politics, government corruption and a host of other issues I thought I knew about, Peter turned to me and asked if I was the president of the United States of America? My answer was a rather confused and puzzled 'no'. Peter then went on to ask if I was a major figure in G8, corporate finance or world banking? Again my answer was 'no', but now I was wondering where this conversation was going. He then asked me that if I were not any of the above, how did I propose to end Third Word Debt, stop government corruption or change international trading relations? I had to confess that I had no solution to any of this, whereupon Peter stated the following rich and powerful words: 'Remember, you cannot change the world; but together you can help us change our world'. At that instant, I gathered that I was being told that none of us are messiahs. We are disciples working for a kingdom beyond our full comprehension and ability, but one that nevertheless relies on our efforts, no matter how small and imperfect they are. We can talk big and do nothing or we can accept our limitations and participate in working towards something truly remarkable. Indeed, the impossible only appears so when we seek to work on our own or attempt to achieve it by ourselves. Hence, we often shrug our shoulders with an air of passivity and resignation that nothing of substance can be achieved. It was the inspirational liberation theologian and martyr Oscar Romero who, while reminding us of our weaknesses and imperfections, exhorted us to radical transforming action. In a famous prayer attributed to Romero, we are urged to understand that we are not messiahs out to achieve the impossible. We are 'builders' of a new world or social order based on justice and respect for human dignity. In this way we are, in fact, co-creators of the possible: 'We may never see the end results, but that is the difference between the master builder and the worker. We are workers, not master builders; ministers, not messiahs. We are prophets of a future not our own.'[11]

Peter Tembo opened my eyes and cured my blindness. For Peter Tembo, hope and possibility permeate every space and corner of our lives. He reminded me that the enemies of hope are passivity, fear of failure, arrogance and a lack of the ability to imagine and dream the possible. He added an objectively grounded and real aspect to insights or dreams that I had considered to be self-delusion and escapism. His vision was utopian only in the sense that it posited the possibility of a better future, a radical human alternative that could only be realised if people dared to dream it. In the same way that Jesus invited people to consider a different order, Peter Tembo helped to undermine my complacency and inertia by suggesting that the existing conditions his community were forced to endure were not eternal or impossible to change. All of the programmes and projects that Peter Tembo identified were, in fact, already present in what the great utopian thinker, Ernst Bloch, referred to as 'anticipatory form' or 'noch-nicht-sein' or 'not-yet-being'.[12] They just needed to be built. The St Lawrence Centre is now one of the main means of empowerment for the people of Misisi, containing a vastly expanded school and special needs centre, a home-based care unit, a computer centre, a medical centre, income generating and agricultural programmes and a host of other inspirational projects that it has been a great privilege for our immersion volunteers to support and serve. That day Peter Tembo taught me a lesson in humility and that I wasn't even asking the right questions, never mind giving the correct answers.

Chapter 4

Irene: A Real Hero in a World of Shallow Celebrities

IN ONE CORNER of the St Lawrence Centre was a four-classroom school building. Opposite it was a special needs centre for fifty-two children who, as well as being born poor beyond imagination, were disabled in some way or other. I found this latter place to be absolutely inspirational. In the affluent West, we find it difficult to deal with people living with disability. Of course, we speak about social inclusion, give awards to those who achieve despite their obvious disadvantage, fit our buildings with wheelchair access, have people do sign language at conferences and on the news, include children with learning difficulties in mainstream education and then clap ourselves on the back as if we have solved the problem of disability. We have not. We have solved *our* problem in dealing with disability. We generally hide it away, or, more correctly, we hide those living with disability away from our sight lest their presence reminds us 'normal' people of our own imperfection and mortality. 'What nonsense!', I hear many people say. 'For God's sake, we even have a Special Olympics at which those with disabilities are able to compete and achieve success in the sporting sphere! We have even changed the terminology so that people who were formerly described as 'handicapped' are now referred to as 'other-abled'. So what's the issue?'

The shallowness of our 'normal' world

There is no doubt that on many fronts progress has indeed been made in this area and that barriers are being pushed. However, we have not yet confronted, never mind solved the problem because the problem is on our side: so-called *normal* society. As a society, we have a clearly defined view of what being 'normal' (and, therefore, accepted) is. Strangely, however, normality, as defined by our affluent society, is very abnormal and, indeed, rare. Normal, as sold to us by the beauty/fitness/fashion industries and celebrity magazines, is a desired, sought after image, a product in which we ourselves have become a commodity that we strive to possess. Look at any glossy magazine or newspaper; glance at any advertising board or advertisements on television; examine how the media portrays 'normal' and you will see that the 'normality' we are aspiring to is beauty or wealth, or preferably both. And when we do not measure up to this image of 'normal' we feel that we are abnormal, that we are less than normal, that we are failures. This causes anxiety, worry, unhappiness and even depression.

People with disabilities subconsciously remind us of our failure to live up to or achieve the type of 'normality' portrayed in the mass media. Many of us fail to be 'body beautiful' or rich beyond imagination like the celebrities whose shallow lives are thrust before us in minute detail and whom we are supposed to imitate. Some seek to 'enter the kingdom' by exposing themselves on *Big Brother* or some other vacuous reality television show. They fail. All they succeed in doing is to reveal their human frailties all the more to audiences gathered by the massive power of the mass media. People with disabilities challenge us by holding up a mirror to us, by forcing us to recognise our own imperfections and weaknesses, by making us consider our mortality. We don't like it so we try to shut them out. Their very presence, even if it is silent, is a threat to us. Our peace is disturbed. They make us feel uncomfortable. We try our best to ignore them, to move them to the margins so that 'normality' is restored.

Jesus and difference

All of this makes what I witnessed on my first visit to the St Lawrence Centre all the more remarkable. In the affluent West, we shun the marginalised, be they people with disabilities, the poor, the homeless, those with mental health problems or prisoners. We pay considerable sums in taxes to various government departments and agencies and other organisations to provide some sort of services for these people so that we are able to continue with our pursuit of happiness and normality without having to meet or embrace those at the margins. Peter McVerry points out, however, that Jesus acted towards the marginalised in precisely the opposite fashion to how we act towards them today. Far from ignoring or shunning them, Jesus reached out to them in a preferential way, which incurred the wrath and disgust of the respectable and the religious authorities of that time. Indeed, McVerry makes this preferential response to the marginalised the very centre of the revelation of Jesus as the Son of God:

The groups that Jesus preferentially reached out to had in common that they were all marginalised in the society to which they belonged. They were marginalised because their society believed that God had marginalised them. The attitudes of society towards them and the way society treated them ensured that they were kept apart, at arm's length ... [Jesus, however] *affirmed their dignity by the way in which he himself related* them. By reaching out to them in a respectful and dignified way, he communicated to them a sense of their own dignity, in the face of the contrary message that they were continually receiving from society. It was as if he said to them: 'Society may not want much to do with you, society may look down on you, but I, and the God from whom I come, we acknowledge your dignity, the same dignity as any other human being in this society.[13]

This sense of affirming the God-given dignity in each person is present among the community of the St Lawrence Centre. Remember, this is a marginalised and forgotten people, crucified by injustice and poverty, with every basic need a priority. Therefore, one of the first things they did when they received some funding from the French Government was build a special needs centre and trained members of their community to become special needs teachers so that the most marginalised of Misisi might have a chance in life. It was at the special needs centre that I met Irene.

Irene: a gift from God to God's children

Irene was the first teacher I met at the special needs centre. She was a young woman from Misisi who had an infectious laugh and a smile that seemed to light up the classroom and radiate a sense of warmth and love all around her. These children were precious to her – as precious as if they were her own. They were vulnerable children from her own community. This is why Irene had decided to become a teacher. In the West today we often praise the professionalism of teachers. We constantly revise our statements of attainment, programmes of study, educational outcomes and learning intentions and opportunities. We stress values such as entrepreneurship, global marketing and economic awareness. It is little wonder that many of us in the West regard education as a vehicle for individual social advancement, as a step up and out, as a means of 'bettering yourself'.

Among the marginalised people who live in the slums of Africa, education is viewed differently. Education is liberation and, in the Third World, that is exactly how it is viewed. Education gives communities a chance to improve their conditions, to lift the community out of poverty. Not that there is anything new and innovative about this notion. After all, it was education that moved Ireland from its impoverished condition following our own holocaust of *An Gorta Mór* a little over one hundred and fifty years ago to the affluent society it is today. Education was also the catalyst that sparked the demand for independence in the former African colonies in the 1950s and 1960s and inspired the civil rights movements in the then segregated southern states in the USA and in

Northern Ireland. The importance of this vision of education cannot be overemphasised or exaggerated. In his Encyclical Letter of 1967, *Populorum Progressio*, Pope Paul VI outlined the situation facing those condemned to live in the margins. His opening statement is as valid today as it was more than four decades ago:

> The development of peoples has the Church's close attention, particularly the development of those peoples who are striving to escape from hunger, misery, endemic diseases and ignorance; of those who are looking for a wider share in the benefits of civilization and a more active improvement of their human qualities; of those who are aiming purposefully at their complete fulfilment ... Today the peoples in hunger are making a dramatic appeal to the peoples blessed with abundance. The Church shudders at this cry of anguish and calls each one to give a loving response of charity to this brother's cry for help.[14]

Crucially, Pope Paul VI placed the solution of this scandal created by and facing the world we live in today not simply on economic development, food aid, new economic and political relations, but equally on education. Thus he stated that 'hunger for education is no less debasing than hunger for food'.[15]

When you step into a school in the Third World you can almost touch the hunger for education. The children, many of whom have to walk miles to school, always arrive early and often depart late. They spend their time in class constantly trying to learn. Education, for them and their communities, is important. It is a way out of poverty. It is a way to empowerment and a better life, but not in the sense that we in the West see education: as an escape from one's background. Rather, in the Third World one cannot be but struck by the desire of the young people not just to improve their own life-chances, but also their wish to improve the conditions of their communities. Ask any class in a basic community school in a slum what they want to be when they leave school and you are struck by the preferences that are offered: 'I want to be a doctor'; 'I want to be a teacher'; 'I want to be a HIV/AIDS counsellor'; 'I want to be a project coordinator'. What they are all actually saying is that they want to make a difference. There is a sense of vocation, of selflessness that is distinctly lacking in the world vision that underpins and is underpinned by the individualism, greed and materialism of our affluent world. These genuinely human values and goals were what led Irene to decide to become a special needs teacher. Irene knew a thing or two about living in a slum and having special needs. Irene, herself, was disabled. She was crippled with polio at birth and had spent her whole life wheelchair-bound. It was uplifting in more senses than one to see the older children every day carrying Irene, sitting in her wheelchair, across the railway lines and over the muddy tracks during the rainy season. She would sing and the children would sing, usually songs about the wonderful things that God had given them, wonderful things indeed, for they had the gift of each other. Irene asked me for one thing when I was leaving for Ireland. 'Aidan, could you bring a manual on special needs education when you return next year? I want

55

to ensure that these children are getting the very best education because they are the best. Isn't that right, children? You are the best!' They smiled, I smiled, she smiled – and she meant it.

The next year I brought a book on special needs education to Lusaka. I went straight to Irene's classroom, knocked on the door and went in fully expecting to be greeted with that laugh and smile. Instead, in front of me stood another teacher. I thought I was in the wrong room. 'I'm sorry,' I said, 'I was looking for Irene's room. Which one is it, please?' The teacher took me aside and quietly informed me that Irene had died in the cholera outbreak two months earlier. I gave her the book, went outside, said a prayer and wept. Irene was twenty-six years of age.

Chapter 5

More Lessons: An Encounter with Br Jacek

WE ALL KNOW that wealth is relative. Br Jacek, a most inspirational religious brother from Poland who works with street children in Lusaka, taught me that. Jacek really goes to the margins and seeks out those who are abandoned; abandoned even by those in the margins. Jacek had arrived in Africa with the full intention of becoming a missionary priest with the White Fathers, but then he encountered some street children. His meeting with these most vulnerable and challenging of children led Jacek to reconsider his options. If he went through with his original plan to become a White Father, he would serve as a missionary priest in one of the numerous mission stations in which this order is based. He would, no doubt, do fantastic work on behalf of whatever impoverished and marginalised community he would find himself in. He would, I am sure, have become a great missionary priest. Yet that life of sacrifice and service was not enough for Jacek Rakowski. No matter how much he wanted to continue his vocation to become a missionary priest, Jacek felt he was being called somewhere else, to another place of Gospel witness. Jacek was called to a most challenging and singular vocation – to embrace perhaps the most marginalised of the marginalised: street children.

Street children: the wretched of the earth

In most countries in the undeveloped world, as well as in the affluent Western world, street children are a despised sub-group, truly part of 'the wretched of the earth'. Unlike children cared for in some of the orphanages we work with in Africa and who receive incredible love and support from the 'aunties' who care for them, street children are very much on their own, or part of a gang of similar victims of poverty and abuse. One can feel great compassion for an orphan in Kabwata Orphanage or a victim of HIV/AIDS in the Sisters of Calcutta Hospice. The plight of these victims of poverty can easily move us to sorrow, empathy and love. Street children are different. Many of the street children are orphans with no one to care for them or who have been cast out by their already struggling stepparents. Some are not actually orphans but have decided to run off to the precarious life in the shadows. All are victims of abuse of some sort or another. They are, as Br Jacek relates, the final result of a process of abuse that leads them to life on the streets. There is nothing easy or attractive about living on the streets or in the sewers or other hidden places beyond the judging eyes of respectable society. I have heard Br Jacek speak at length to groups of immersion volunteers about the reality of street life on a number of occasions. It is a heart-breaking and harrowing account. Jacek says that you will encounter street children in the most hidden and invisible of places. Sometimes you will find them at sewage ponds, plunging their hands into the dark brown sludge, gathering fistfuls of human excrement and stuffing it into small plastic bottles or other containers. They are making Jenkem, a potent, disgusting, noxious substance made from fermented human sewage. They will leave it for a week or so to ferment, regularly tapping the bottles on the ground, taking care to allow enough space for methane to form at the top. For those too poor to buy glue or too afraid to steal petrol, Jenkem is a way of getting high and forgetting the world for an hour or so.

Street kids are despised as thieves, often because they do indeed steal. If they are caught stealing, they will often be severely beaten. Sometimes the police will intervene to stop this, at other times they look the other way. Sometimes they join in. In countries where poverty is rife and in which the vast majority of the people are living at the very margins of survival, it is often the poorest of the poor, the most vulnerable of the vulnerable, who are seen as a problem, an embarrassment, a threat. They beg, they smell, they sniff solvents ('Stika' or 'Jenkem') to escape the harsh realities of their harsh lives. They make you feel uncomfortable, guilty and fearful so you turn your head away so that you don't have to do anything about it. If they do not exist then they are not a problem – at least not your problem. It is all too easy to fall in love with the children in an orphanage or feel compassion for victims of hunger, illness and poverty. These 'poor unfortunates' fall into the category of what the Victorians called 'the deserving poor': those who are innocent of causing their own misery and, therefore, 'deserving' of our charity, our compassion, our action. There is nothing nice, 'deserving' or appealing about street children – except their humanity. They have to join a gang to survive and do unspeakable things (or allow such things to be done to them) to remain in the gang. Life must indeed be awful if this is the best option.

Jesus and outsiders

How did Jesus react when he met with the 'undeserving' poor or marginalised? Certainly there were many who fell into this category: sinners, tax collectors, sick people, the disabled, the materially poor, outsiders and many others. They were unworthy of God's love and, therefore, of respectable society's compassion. Like the street children of the Developing World they were worthy only of the sewers and hidden places they lived in, the life *they* had chosen. That is only fair.

Yet the God who Jesus revealed to us (and was revealed to us through Jesus) is *unfair*. This God does not give us an easy way out through being charitable to those who deserve our charity and compassion. God does not demand us to be fair. Instead God demands *justice* from us. He commands us to look beyond the appearance, the conditions, the actions and lifestyles of the despised 'undeserving' marginalised and to recognise and affirm their God-given human dignity. We must cease to treat them as things, as non-persons, and see them instead as our fellow brothers and sisters of immense and infinite value and worth. Peter McVerry again is instructive on this. According to McVerry, the God who is fair is relatively easy to deal with because He is predictable: keep the Law and He will reward you; don't keep the Law and He will punish you. This was the God of the Pharisees and one whom many of us were taught to obey and fear lest we live uncaring and unworthy lives and earn His wrath. This is also the God of charity whose favour we will earn by helping those deserving victims of circumstances not of their own making. And so we help those whom this God would wish us to help. Yet McVerry shows us that this is not the God of justice who is, in fact, totally *unfair*. In the Parable of the Labourers at the Vineyard, for example, we are shown a God whose sense of justice conflicts with our sense of fair play. Jesus instructs the disciples as follows:

> The Kingdom of heaven is like this. Once there was a man who went out early in the morning to hire some men to work in his vineyard. He agreed to pay them the regular wage, a silver coin a day, and sent them to work in his vineyard. He went out again to the market place at nine o'clock and saw some men standing there doing nothing, so he told them, 'You also go and work in the vineyard, and I will pay you a fair wage.' So they went. Then at twelve o'clock and again at three o'clock he did the same thing. It was nearly five o'clock when he went to the market place and saw some other men still standing there. 'Why are you wasting the whole day here doing nothing?' he asked them. 'No one hired us,' they answered. 'Well, then, you also go and work in the vineyard,' he told them. When evening came, the owner told his foreman, 'Call the workers and pay them their wages, starting with those who were hired last and ending with those who were hired first.' The men who had begun to work at five o'clock were paid a silver coin each. So when the men who were the first to be hired came to be paid, they thought they would

get more; but they too were given a silver coin each. They took their money and started grumbling against the employer. 'These men who were hired last worked only one hour,' they said, 'while we put up with a whole day's work in the hot sun – yet you paid them the same as you paid us!'

'Listen, friend,' the owner answered one of them, 'I have not cheated you. After all, you agreed to do a day's work for one silver coin. Now take your pay and go home. I want to give this man who was hired last as much as I have given you. Don't I have the right to do as I wish with my own money? Or are you jealous because I am generous?' And Jesus concluded, 'So those who are last will be first, and those who are first will be last.'

(Matthew 20:1-6)

McVerry tells us that through this parable (and other such lessons as the Parable of the Prodigal Son and the story of the Woman Caught in Adultery) that we are compelled by this God who does not condemn and who is justice to reach out to those in need unconditionally, non-judgementally and 'unrestricted by individual, personal moral choices' (McVerry, p. xx). The only ones judged in this relationship is us and the spirit of our reaching out. Do we act like the Pharisees, urging rigid adherence or duty to the Law, and hence judge those who are, therefore, objects of our charity and pity; or do we reach out as Jesus instructed us, in an unconditional sense, expecting no reward, and, indeed, putting ourselves as servants to others? We are compelled to reach out to those whom society despises, to commit ourselves to those who have been pushed to the margins by a judging and (apparently) fair society. McVerry challenges us thus:

> [We must] seek to build a society whose economic, social and political structures and policies are shaped by a radical concern for those in need, *whether we consider them deserving or not.* To believe in a God who has a passionate concern for those on the margins compels us to struggle to create a society which has a passionate concern for those on the margins. To believe in a God who does not condemn compels us to struggle to create a society which does not condemn.[16]

Of course, this goes against every way we have been taught to think and act. It is not sufficient to simply help those on the margins; we must seek to create a society based on the needs of those very people. The implications for us in the affluent world should not be shunned or ignored. If we are really serious about justice and not simply charity, we have to be clear in our understanding that we will have to be unlike the labourers in the vineyard who complained about the unfairness of it all. It is not sufficient to work for the poor if we don't work to overcome the system that makes and keeps them poor. The new society towards which immersion points will also necessarily involve the abolition of our wasteful consumerist lifestyle. In this radical transformation, it is not just the Bill Gateses of this world who will find their wealth and lifestyle changed, all of us have to question our own standard of living if we truly desire justice for the marginalised.

You, me and Bill Gates

'And they think that you, as a *muzungu*, are just like Bill Gates', said Br Jacek when asked how the street children viewed us. I thought Br Jacek must be using a touch of exaggeration here, after all, Bill Gates is wealthy and Aidan Donaldson is not. Bill Gates has an income in excess of the entire wealth of dozens of Third World countries and Aidan Donaldson is a teacher who has an acceptable income in Ireland. Surely I am closer in terms of income to those who live in the margins than to the Bill Gateses of this world? My weekly income may be several hundreds of pounds in excess of the meagre sum on which the poor in the slums, shanty towns and *favelas* of Africa, India and Latin America are forced to seek out survival, but my salary pales in comparison to the earnings of the super-rich David Beckham, Christiano Ronaldo, Didier Drogba and a host of other international footballers and sports persons, as well as famous pop stars, models, actors and others who are paid quite incredible sums of money and who earn more in one week than I earn in years. So how can I have anything in common with people like that? Br Jacek hit us with a few home truths that have changed my view on how those at the margins view us. For those who live in absolute poverty – the overwhelming majority of which whose sole 'crime' is to have been born in Africa, Latin America, India and those other places that make up the Third World – we have so much more in common with Bill than those in the margins have with us. And they are right. Bill, you, the reader, or I will not die due to a lack of clean water. We will not have to experience the awfulness of listening to our children crying because we have no money for food, nor will we watch them suffer because we cannot afford to pay for basic medicines. The life-chances of our children will not be held back because we cannot pay for their education. All of these things that we take for granted and presume everybody has access to lie far beyond the dreams of so many millions of people in the world. Our world is not their world. The slums of Kibera and Misisi bear witness to that simple truth. We have to change that truth.

Listening to Jacek's impassioned plea on behalf of the poor would move anyone to action. So it was no surprise, therefore, that we asked him at the end of his talk if there was something we could do to help the street children he worked with. Perhaps we were asking for something 'easy' to do such as sponsor a project that would make a difference for the street children in the Home of Hope. However, Jacek does not do 'easy'. 'Okay, let's think about this', said Jacek. Then he paused for a minute before looking directly at each of us and giving us a real challenge that would make a difference to us. Jacek threw down the gauntlet:

If you saw your very own brother laying at the side of the road in much the condition of a street child you would most certainly do everything in your power to help him. Wouldn't you? Of course you would. After all, he is your brother. It is only natural to help him. Even if you had argued and fallen out with your brother, even if you had not spoken with him or seen him in years, you would still recognise him as your very own brother who is in need and you would help him no matter the cost. Now, this is what I want you to do. I want you to recognise the humanity in everyone you meet, no matter who they are or how they look. I want you not to judge when you meet someone on the streets or in the margins. I want you to reach out to them. I want you not to ignore them and walk past them. I want you to see them as your very own brother or sister.

Br Jacek certainly doesn't make things easy for you. How many times do we come across a person begging on the streets of Belfast or Dublin and refuse to see them or acknowledge their presence or even existence? Do we see some young person sniffing glue and judge him/her as 'a waste of space', as someone to be avoided and condemned? Does social embarrassment, conditioning or even fear make us look the other way lest we establish eye contact and feel that we should recognise them as real living persons, as fully a person as you and I? Sometimes it is easier to go up to a beggar, an orphan, a person suffering from HIV/AIDS, a grandparent carer or any other victim of poverty in the undeveloped world and give them a hug, food, money or whatever else we feel they need than it is to sit down with someone suffering exactly the same form of neglect in our own neighbourhoods and communities in Ireland and ask how life is with them. It is much easier to place a coin in the polystyrene cup of a homeless person than it is to ask them their name. If we find out what their name is and how they are then we may have to treat them as our brother and sister. Br Jacek doesn't let us give money and then move on. Jacek makes us turn our eyes away from the road or pavement and look directly into the eyes of someone in the margins. He makes us look into a mirror and see ourselves. Jacek is truly remarkable.

Confronting the False World of Consumerism

Chapter 6

'Bubbles'

'BUBBLES' ARE QUITE strange and scary places. They insulate you against reality; they disguise the world as it really is and seek to assure you that there is nothing wrong, unfamiliar or even different about it. 'Bubbles' allow you to live a Western consumerist lifestyle even though you are in the Developing World. In short, 'bubbles' are the greatest invention and celebration of the materialist world in which we live. By 'bubbles' I mean shopping centres: those great cathedrals of consumer capitalism located in every city in the world and in which the rich and affluent go to look, idolise, worship and be confirmed in their salvation (economic and social salvation at least). The use of religious language and symbolism here is quite deliberate. Stepping into any of the 'bubbles' in Lusaka one is struck by a number of familiar yet peculiar things. All of the elements one expects to find in a modern shopping centre in the Developed World are there in their uniform, identical and bland forms: restaurants, coffee shops, fast food outlets, designer fashion outlets, shops selling the latest computers, plasma televisions, mobile phones and every other 'must-have' gadget that we are told we must possess.

Taking centre stage in these 'bubbles' are the banks and financial centres without which none of the above would be possible. One is struck by the omnipresence of armed soldiers and police around these places. At one level they may be seen as some sort of assurance that the effective and smooth transfer of money and commerce can take place without the risk of criminals (or even desperate and needy people) attempting to short-cut their way to the salvation of riches without having to go through the different levels of social and economic initiation. It would be most distasteful and immoral if people motivated by greed actually attempted to steal the fruits of a system based on, well, greed. My own feeling is that the presence of armed forces around such centres, while acting as a security service for the banks, shops and other retail enterprises, has a much more serious and important function and purpose. Their very presence is a statement and warning that no poor person, street orphan, beggar or 'social embarrassment', i.e. one who would upset the consumers, shall enter the kingdom. If they do so, they should be prepared to be judged.

Sometimes, when I have to visit a 'bubble', for example to access internet facilities, change money or get medication for someone in the immersion group, I might spend some time over a coffee. The world inside the 'bubble' is so unlike the world you encounter outside of it. Usually, I will walk from the hostel to the main road to get a minibus. From the time you leave the hostel until you reach the bus stop (a short distance of no more than eight hundred metres) you become very aware that *bazungu* are not expected to walk. Forget the taxis that will race towards you in the expectation of getting a fare because a *muzungu* does not walk, abandon the comfort and perceived security and get on a minibus instead. You sit with people there and they will smile and say 'hello'. They will affirm your humanity.

Encounters in a 'bubble'

One day a couple of years ago, my school principal, Kevin Burke, and I went to a craft market beside a small or 'semi-bubble' called North Mead (a couple of shops, a pharmacy, bars/restaurants/fast food outlets, a tacky night club and a petrol station) to buy a few presents for family and friends back in Ireland. It was coming towards the last day or two of this particular immersion experience, that very precious time when you are entering closure. There was lots to do and not enough time. After an hour or so in the craft market we decided that we had had enough of haggling, buying and packing 'going home' things, so we moved across the road to a shop which had a small coffee area attached to it. The shop, like most shops in Zambia, was owned by a very industrious Indian, who was moving around his premises ensuring that all was well. Kevin and I wanted to sit together, have a coffee and reflect on what immersion was doing to us; to explore the personal change that each immersion brings. The shop to which we were going was across the storm drains and a sort of 'no man's land' of approximately fifty metres, which separates the tourist 'buying presents' zone of the craft market from the small consumer zone. During the day this space is inhabited by street vendors and beggars all trying to earn enough to sustain the daily hand-to-mouth existence that means survival for so many in the Developing World. At night this space is occupied by an even sadder and more tragic group of people: those young women and girls who are so desperate that they sell their sole possession – themselves – to those who will pay for their use as sexual objects. Many of the men who beg during the day spend the pittance they are given on Shake-Shake: a rather vile looking and, for me, unpleasant tasting maize drink, which is brewed throughout much of sub-Saharan Africa. If you walk through any shanty town in Africa anytime after dawn, you will be struck by the noise emanating from the beer halls and the sight of men – always men – staggering out of the shacks, bearing such apparently grandiose names as The Manchester United Tavern, The Lusaka Inn, The Victoria Falls, and asking *bazungu* for 'money for Shake-Shake'. We can all be too judgemental and righteous in such situations. I confess that I have been all too often. When I see the squalor the people of the slums live in and witness the inspirational efforts of so many ordinary yet heroic people of those very same slums to try to improve the living conditions I often become angry and indignant. I find myself asking, in fact, demanding: 'Why do they waste their money on drink? Why do they not use whatever they are given or earn to feed their families? Why are they so selfish?' It was Kevin who stopped one of my self-righteous rants after witnessing precisely one such scenario at eight o'clock in the morning in the middle of Misisi when he pointed out that if I lived in such conditions and without hope then, perhaps, I too might wish to put my head in some other place. Since we in the West live in a 'global bubble', we should be careful before we judge those whose sole way of dealing with existence is to put their heads somewhere else. A man called James was one of them.

Kevin and I met James at the bottom of the steps that lead from the edge of the 'no man's land' up to the citadel of the 'semi-bubble': the shopping zone. Because North Mead is not a fully-fledged 'bubble', not having any banks, ATMs, plush restaurants or high-class shops, there isn't a great concentration of whites, rich Africans and affluent others. Also, there is no 'heavy' security there. I like North Mead because if you have to buy essentials there you can do so without having the hassle of entering the 'matrix' of a real 'bubble', like Manda Hill or Arcades. James was old – at least in Zambian terms. He had two jaundiced eyes, possibly the result of hepatitis or HIV. He coughed a lot (perhaps TB) as he nursed his carton of Shake-Shake. He smiled at Kevin and me as we walked past him. 'Hey *bazungu*, what land do you come from? How is life in your country?' He asked this in a most friendly and genuine fashion. He just wanted to know who we were, where we were from, to share our stories, to acknowledge and celebrate our common humanity. We smiled back and bade him *'mula bwanji'* in our best Nyanga.

The very idea of two *bazungu* using his language must have intrigued James and curiosity got the better of him. He hobbled up the steps, into the bar area and sat down beside Kevin and me. One quickly gets used to the smell of poverty in Africa and James was poor. He was also a man and a very interesting and wise man at that. He spoke four languages, as well as English, and he had worked in the Copper Belt during better times in Zambia. Now he had returned to Lusaka to a township for whatever time he had left. He showed a remarkable grasp of international politics and was giving a lecture to his spellbound audience of two white men on African politics during the Cold War when the owner of the shop saw him. He was not happy. James had invaded a zone from which he and his type were banned. He was, in the owner's eyes, annoying the *bazungu*, which is bad for business. Before we had time to say anything, two shop assistants, both African, bundled James out the door and threw him down the steps. The owner apologised to us and assured us on our leaving that we would not be bothered with such people again. All we could do was sit with James as he resignedly took up his place once again on the other side of 'no man's land' from which he had had the audacity to escape, even if briefly, to talk to two other people. As he wiped the blood from his cuts he continued telling his story, berating the global injustice of which he is most certainly a victim, as we had just witnessed. We gave him some money and apologised for our whiteness, which had caused his injuries. He thanked us and wished us '*salani bweno*' or 'safe journey'. We wished him 'good life' and left feeling angry for what had happened, our pathetic response and our inadequacy in failing to stop yet another injustice being delivered onto this man. The world is indeed a cruel, harsh and unjust place – especially for people such as James.

Chapter 7

The Inhumanity of our Modern Human Society

LET US PAUSE for a moment and step back to consider the world we live in, the world we have created. It is a cruel, uncaring and unjust place. It is the very antithesis of a world in which humans can come truly alive with and for each other, a world in which we recognise ourselves in the other. It is a world in which we have lost (or are in danger of losing) our ability to be human. How else can we explain the apparent indifference to the suffering of so many people throughout the world, whose only crime is to have been born in the abject poverty that persists throughout the so-called Developing World? As selfishness and a sense of disconnection from others become increasingly part of the human condition in the affluent world, many have developed a remarkable ability to become completely uninterested in and detached from the truly horrific and criminal. Examine the reaction of the world to the on-going torture and annihilation of the people of Darfur in Sudan. Over the past number of years, the people of the southern region in that country have been suffering what is effectively a genocide inflicted on them by the Government of Sudan's armed forces, aided by the Janjaweed (literally 'devils on horseback') militia. These government-sponsored forces are aptly named as they, and the regular army, systematically use rape as a weapon of terror in their campaign of brutalisation, torture and suppression of the people of Darfur. Human rights observers, as well as official United Nations reports, have calculated that, so far, some two hundred and fifty thousand people of the region have been killed and more than two million displaced in the war against the innocent. The situation is being monitored, reported on and condemned, but there has still been no action from the world community to put an end to such barbarity. The plight of the victims – played out on twenty-four-hour satellite television – cries out to the very heavens for justice. In the West, the inaction of the rich and powerful, as well as the silence of many others, is taken by the perpetrators as indifference and even encouragement. In our silence lies our compliance and guilt.

Let us ponder on some statistics:
- The six richest people in the world own more than the six hundred million poorest combined.
- The three hundred richest people in the world own more of the world's wealth than half of humanity.
- We spend thirty times more on military expenditure than on international development.
- One million tons of food is thrown out each year in Europe alone.
- In the US they spend five times more on cosmetics than on helping the world's poor.
- Thirty thousand African children will die today.[17]

For me, the last statistic illustrates just how inhuman and detached from human suffering our society has become. As you read this there are thirty thousand African children who are alive today but will be dead by tomorrow.[18] There is nothing unusual or even remarkable about this since each and every single day some thirty thousand children in Africa die. Let us put this statistic into context. Thirty thousand deaths roughly equates to the following:

- Ten times the number of those who died over three decades of the recent Northern Ireland conflict.
- The same number of those (approximately nine hundred thousand) who perished in the 1994 one hundred-day genocide in Rwanda dying each month.
- Approximately the same number of people who died in the Irish Famine perishing every month.
- The equivalent of the Holocaust committed by the Nazis repeated every seven months.

'Never again would such crimes against humanity be allowed to happen' – so universally stated the voice of world opinion after the Holocaust of the Second World War. Yet life is indeed cheap in Africa and much of the rest of the world. The world is no longer such a big place in which unspeakable disasters, horrors and suffering can be inflicted on others without our knowing and, ultimately, our acceptance. The communications revolution of the past two decades – as evidenced by the omnipresence (and all-pervasive influence) of twenty-four-hour satellite television channels, the internet and mobile phones – means that we can no longer claim that we do not know what is happening in the world. For many people, especially in the Developed World, it is not a case of not knowing; rather it is simply a case of not caring or at the very least feeling so disempowered or detached from what is happening that making a difference doesn't seem to be an option. Not that one should be surprised at this; after all, we live in a world bombarded by and, ultimately, moulded by a diet of 'reality' television, advertising and consumerism. Writing almost forty years ago, the Romanian-born philosopher, Lucien Goldmann, prophetically expressed the effects of the brutalisation and manipulation of consciousness inherent in consumerist culture:

> The absolute, passive consumer earning his living as a simple performer of tasks in order to buy himself gadgets: the *Club Mediterrannée* of thought – this is the great threat which looms large on the horizon. Something more subtle and pernicious has replaced the external constraint of fascism and the concentration camps: brutalisation, brain-washing, corruption through income, holidays, the effects of the mass-media and advertising.[19]

Critical consciousness, the ability to grasp, understand, reflect upon and make judgements on situations that we encounter, has been replaced by what Herbert Marcuse called 'the consciousness of the happy robot'.[20] The staggering degree to which modern humankind has embraced and shaped its own powerlessness can be illustrated by the fact that not only do more people tune into *Big Brother* every day than watch the news, but more people vote on who they wish to be evicted from the Big Brother House, something they actually have to pay for, than exercise their franchise in voting in a general election. With such inverted values, disconnection and distorted world vision, it is little wonder that the plight of those dying in such vast numbers throughout the undeveloped world does not appear on the West's radar of concern. Those who live in the margins exist only in the margins of the consciousness and conscience of the world.

In the affluent world, at least these children and their parents would have a death certificate. It might read 'Cause of Death: malaria/AIDS/typhoid/yellow fever/ hunger' or any other of the host of diseases and other ailments that blight the Third World. However, one cause of death in Africa would be missing: 'old age'. This omission is glaringly obvious. The average life expectancy in much of sub-Saharan Africa, for example, is now under forty years of age – and falling. The 'missing generation' in Africa, i.e. that generation of parents that bridges the gap between children and grandparents, is recognisable to any visitor or even tourist who strays outside the comfort zone of the hotel, shopping complex or safari experience. Enter a township in a sprawling urban area or a rural village and you will be amazed and humbled to witness a grandmother unquestioningly and lovingly devoting all of her energy to providing for a family of orphans. This type of care in the so-called Developed World would be given to a single child through healthcare, education and social services. Similarly, it is both deeply moving and awe-inspiring to see a child often as young as twelve or thirteen (and generally female) taking on the role of mother and father to provide a future for her younger siblings – without any help from outside agencies or local services.

You will not read 'cause of death' on any death certificate because the people who die in the margins do not receive a piece of paper acknowledging the fact of their death, never mind the cause of their passing. They are not important enough to get even that recognition. Each of these people who die is a non-person, simply a statistic or figure recorded on a graph or chart in a report or an article of interest. Their deaths will not move powerful nations to action or the conscience of the affluent to question the lifestyle or economic system that causes their deaths. Like the victims of any other holocaust or human disaster, they had names, a family which adored them, which loved them, which valued them and which now grieves for them and misses them deeply. Their family may have had ambitions and dreams for them. But they are non-persons; they do not have a birth certificate and, consequently, they will not be issued with a death certificate. They did not exist, therefore they could not have died. It is quite bizarre how the media instead choose to focus on the latest escapade of some pop star. We live in a world that does not have news, just gossip; a world without heroes or role models, just celebrities.

The true cause of death of all of those deemed as non-persons in the world is much more simple and uncomplicated than what the media tells us. They died of one single, curable man-made disease: poverty. There is nothing natural about poverty. The old colonial imperialistic myth that the Third World is in a state of extreme deprivation because of a lack of natural or human resources is precisely that – a colonial imperialist myth and a falsehood that reinforces racial stereotypes, masks the real underlying causes of poverty, including historical and structural injustices, exploitative socio-economic relationships and neo-colonialism, and ignores the only solution to the inhuman misery that constitutes daily life (and death) for much of the world's population: justice. Not least of the injustices that those who suffer from poverty have to endure under the myth of 'natural poverty' is that many in the Developed World blame the victims for the crimes inflicted on them. Modern consumerist society denigrates and mocks their culture, it seeks to make them feel inferior and force them to adopt the 'Western way', it denies responsibility for the poverty the consumerist society in the global north has created and it refuses to make any redress for the wrongs it has done. Consumerist society seeks to make those in the Third World conform to its own image and likeness through the all-encompassing process of globalisation, the extension of multinational economic structures and the imposition of dominant Western cultural models into the life fabric of the Developing World.

The process by which all alternative world visions, social structures, cultural identities and political and economic relations are, first of all, undermined, then destroyed and, finally, replaced by a foreign and closed social order is absolutely essential for the creation of a single social system that is required for the ceaseless expansion and continual regeneration of the consumer society. To use the celebrated description of the American sociologist George Ritzer, this 'McDonaldisation' of the world is a fundamental and vital element in consumer capitalism's attempt to reshape every aspect of social living in its own image: that of the monistic New World Order.[21] Whatever does not conform to the limited form of Weberian rationality, to the primacy of economic motives, to the inherently antihuman processes of exploitation and alienation – in short, to the commodification of human existence – is viewed as suspect and must be eliminated. All of the truly human dimensions and expressions of human living – language, culture, music, joy, love, happiness, sorrow, community – are being systematically replaced by a bland and pernicious secularist and materialistic individualism, which enables the inhuman mechanisms of consumer society (and its consequences) to appear as natural, inexorable and right. Everything is transformed into its opposite: being is turned into having; love into desire; community into an association of mutually self-absorbed individuals; sharing into possession; 'we' into 'I'; 'you' – in truth God's reflection and an extension of myself – now a threatening competitor; truth into deceit; action into passivity; respect into jealousy; justice into class rule; God into material goods. Our Western inverted and confused world, created by greed, is outlined in a thought-provoking passage by the great German political philosopher, Karl Marx. Marx points out that the 'divine power' of money in our acquisitive society transforms all human and natural qualities into their opposites and produces a most bizarre and, in fact, impossible world –

a world which we all inhabit. Quoting Mephistopheles from Goethe's Faust, Marx showed how, even in the early emerging consumer society, the reduction of everything to money inverts and distorts reality. Thus, when Mephistopheles states, 'Six stallions, I can afford. Is not their strength my property? I tear along, a sporting lord, as if their legs belong to me',[22] Marx points out that here what one *has* or can *purchase*, one *is* or can *be*.

Chapter 8

The Magical Power of Money

CAN MONEY REALLY change everything? Can it make a lame man walk, a blind man see or an ugly man attractive? In fact, it can. On one of my immersion experiences in Zambia I witnessed a very sad, disturbing and distasteful episode that was a clear illustration of the power and destructive nature of money. It demonstrated to me just how correct the descriptions of Goethe and Marx of the transforming, dehumanising and enslaving effects of money are.

It was a warm August day in Lusaka, at least warm for this red-haired and freckle-faced *muzungu* from Ireland. It was around twenty-eight degrees and, given that July and August are the coolest months in Zambia, I thought I had a bit of cheek to complain about the heat to the guys squeezed on top of each other as the minibus hurtled down the Great East Road. Travelling on public transport is easily the best way of encountering people and embracing the immersion spirit. It is about abandoning all of your Western phobias about personal space, avoiding eye contact, touch and so on and letting go of just about every barrier our Western lifestyle has forced us to adopt. On a minibus everyone is the same. There is no first class or the isolated 'security' of the taxi or private car. No, this is authentic transport in Africa: people everywhere, going somewhere, trying to get on with living or, at least, surviving.

You are surrounded by ordinary people from every walk of life, each on their own journey: children going home from school; women bringing some food or other goods back from a market; men going to/returning from work while others, smartly dressed but perhaps wearing the only decent pair of shoes and clothes that their entire family possesses, going into town in the never-ending desperate search for a day's work so that their family might have some food tomorrow. You very quickly notice the smell of people when you travel on a minibus. Not the smell of aftershave or perfume, which pervades the atmosphere when you enter someone's personal space in the West. Not even the smell of cheap deodorant to disguise the smell of body odour. In a land where 80 per cent of the population are living on less than one dollar per day, such trivial things as soap and cosmetics are not merely viewed as luxuries, they are impossibilities. Yet there is something good about being aware of the presence of the other through the sense of smell. It affirms the humanity, frailty, incompleteness and reality of each of us. The false world of cosmetics has a purpose other than masking the unpleasant odours of day-to-day living. Cosmetics also send out a message about how much material wealth the wearer either possesses or is prepared to spend on such things, with the wealthy able to buy designer brands to suit their designer lifestyle while those who are poor (in relative terms, at least) able only to buy the cheaper supermarket brands. The shallowness and inversion of values that dominates Western culture can be attested to the fact that in the US, more than five times the amount is spent on cosmetics than helping the world's poor, as well as thirty times more on military expenditure than international development.[23]

I got off the minibus at a brand new, glitzy shopping centre – one of those 'bubbles' in which the rich and privileged can go to 'worship' the gods of consumer capitalism and in which their status as 'elect' is confirmed by their very entry into such elevated places. Perhaps it is the religion teacher or scholastic philosopher in me, but I am fascinated by the parallels that can be drawn between some religious beliefs and such places. The Kingdom of God has most certainly been replaced – both physically and in the minds and aspirations of those who enter this strange kingdom – by the Kingdom of Consumerism with its attendant 'cathedrals' and rituals. There also appears to be strong pseudo-Calvinist doctrines in evidence. One of the most distinctive teachings of the Swiss reformer was the doctrine of predestination and the separation of humankind into those who will be saved ('the Elect') and those who will not ('the Damned').[24] According to Calvin, God knows in advance who will be saved and who will be damned. Furthermore, 'the Elect' know themselves to be saved and recognise this state of grace in others. An interesting, although somewhat modified process can be witnessed in the new Kingdom of Consumerism among the worshippers there. The whites – 'the Elect', who are confirmed as such by the colour of their skin (which in turn is quite a sure indication of the fact that they have wealth) – are welcomed into the 'kingdom' irrespective of their dress and appearance. With money and opulence comes power and access. The security guards will look beyond even the most scruffy and unshaven backpacking *muzungu* to ensure that no street child or beggar will slip into the 'cathedral' and spoil the purity of the social and economic exchange that is taking place there.

If the *muzungu* is confirmed in his/her salvation by the colour of his/her skin, how do the other 'worshippers' gain access? One of the other groups that one sees in such 'bubbles' are those of Indian origin. Originally brought to colonies in eastern and southern Africa by the British as labourers, this community, despite its relatively small size, is very important in the commerce of numerous countries throughout sub-Saharan Africa. Due to its economic importance, the Indian community has gained considerable wealth and so it is not surprising that you will see their presence in the shopping malls in Lusaka and cities throughout southern Africa. They stand out by their very distinctive Indian dress and appearance. Their wealth has saved them and they can, and frequently do, enter the 'cathedral'.

The other group which one encounters in such places are the rich blacks who have, in economic terms, 'made it'. This group consists of the richest 10 per cent of the Zambian population (as is the case in most Third World countries), who have escaped the grinding poverty that crushes the vast majority of the people. They are confirmed in their 'elect' status not just by their economic ability to purchase the consumer goods and Western lifestyle, which is the very *raison d'être* for the existence of such centres; this group affirms its membership of the elite by adopting all sorts of Western cultural habits including clothing, hairstyles and music, as well as developing a Western way of looking at the world, including looking at themselves. The world of Pepsi and Coke, of McDonald's and Burger King, of Gucci and Armani and of Manchester United and Chelsea can be found in the strangest places.

There is nothing new or unusual about this behaviour. Throughout human history there seems to be a constant trend among those who have escaped the worst excesses of oppression and exploitation through social advancement to copy the social and cultural mores of their oppressors. This is done in the (often vain) hope that they might leave behind their subjugation and rise out of their former imposed station to become an accepted member of the elite. It is also interesting to note that in ancient Rome, the most harsh slave owners were often former slaves themselves. A well-off slave would buy his own slave whom he would hire out.

Such aspirations are not limited to the Developing World or the ancient one. In affluent Western society, one can witness how many of those who have emerged out of and 'beyond' their social class try to re-invent themselves. They do so in an attempt to fit into their new social world and to be accepted by the social group to which they aspire and with whom they now identify. Similarly, in Celtic Tiger Ireland, it was (and still is) not uncommon to meet people who 'bought the whole package', which means fully embracing and celebrating consumerism, materialism and greed. This comes at a price, however, as it includes abandoning the traditional Irish communal values of extended family, community, welcoming the stranger and caring for the old, the sick and the lonely. The long-standing, almost unconscious siding with the marginalised and oppressed throughout the world (almost certainly as a result of our own country's history and collective memory) may also no longer be taken as a given, because individualism and materialism weaken the inclination to solidarity, social justice and the promotion of the common good. Furthermore, recent social trends may indicate not just a downturn in religious practice, but also a privatising of religion. This latter trend is at least as problematic and challenging to the Church in Ireland today as a downright rejection of Christianity and its values. When religion ceases to lead to action, it loses its essentially vocational and transformational nature. It becomes a private duty to be carried out without leading the person to go into the world and live out the exhortation at the end of Mass, 'Go in peace to love and serve the Lord'. The challenge to live out the Gospel in the world, to make the Eucharist and the sacrifice of Jesus recreated at Mass part of our lives, is rendered safe and, ultimately, meaningless by privatised observance of ritual. It allows life to go on without disturbing the peace. And, for God's sake, let us not take that radical social Gospel in the story of the Final Judgement (Matthew 25:31-45), in which we are exhorted, indeed *commanded*, to feed the hungry, tend the sick, visit and care for the forgotten, too seriously. Nor let us take too seriously the parable of the Good Samaritan (Luke 10:25-37) in which we discover that our neighbour may be those whom we distrust, despise and view as outsiders. As for the story of the Rich Young Man (Mark 10:17-31), in which Jesus tells him to sell all he has, give it to the poor and only then can he follow him, surely Jesus didn't really mean that this is what we too must do? Otherwise, if we did think about them seriously, we might encounter some difficult questions about our own lifestyle and priorities, our vision of the world and our relationships with others.

Inside the 'bubble'

My purpose for going to the shopping centre was to change money. I prefer to avoid these artificial places as much as I can, but on occasions when I need to change large sums of money these centres can provide a measure of security that makes the use of their facilities worthwhile and sensible. Entering the complex from the minibus stop, I was conscious that I was the only *muzungu* to have opted for that means of transport. There were a number of Africans who got off the minibus who were also coming into the shopping centre from that direction: young girls in their restaurant uniforms hurrying to work; young lads heading towards the shopping outlets; older women and men, impeccably dressed, going to their places of employment in the offices and commercial business centres. They all had a number of things in common with each other: they worked in one of the most highly desired shopping zones in Lusaka, with its air-conditioning, manicured garden surrounds, polished colonnades and everything else necessary to make an affluent consumer feel quite at home. They would also have a first-hand view of what the world of globalised capitalism promises, with the mock architecture, fetching floral displays (mostly artificial), the all-pervading and (deliberately) forgettable elevator music and the omnipresent satellite television and advertising monitors, as they go about their daily job of servicing the needs of the affluent. The contrast between the world they live in – the slums and compounds of Lusaka – and the world they work in truly is a microcosm of the world today.

Some people in such shopping centres provide a completely de-humanising service as they seek to survive, a service which, it seems, is not without takers. I had completed my currency exchange without any difficulty and found that I had some time to kill before being joined by Br John McCourt, so I strolled around the shopping malls for a while until I came to a rather flashy, overstated and lavish bar/restaurant that has become a magnet for the well-off. It was the middle of the afternoon and the place was quiet. Lunch had just finished and the restaurant staff were tidying up. I decided that the bar might be a quiet place to sit for thirty minutes or so until Br John arrived. I walked into the bar, receiving the usual friendly greeting from the security man at the entrance. The sign on the door informed me that 'the management reserves the right to restrict entrance to those not properly dressed'. I was, despite my somewhat casual and scruffy attire, properly dressed. My *muzungu* skin saw to that.

I sat down at a table in the bar and a waiter came down very quickly. I asked for a glass of beer. I then noticed a group of young girls aged around fifteen to eighteen years of age ... and they noticed me. They were all very attractive, wearing bright, tight-fitting Western clothes and were heavily made-up beyond their years. I had been in Africa often enough to know how these girls make their money and understood the sad reality of why they do so. They had also noticed that I was on my own. The waiter arrived with my drink and I asked him to bring me a soft drink with ice. I set this opposite me to suggest that I was awaiting someone who had, perhaps, gone to the bathroom or whose arrival was imminent. It is sad that I had to buy a drink for an imaginary friend so that these young women – in reality scarcely beyond childhood – would not approach me. I sat wishing that I could talk to them and ask them their names and who they were. I wanted to tell them not to do what they were doing and suggest that they should try to improve their lives through education, empowerment and community action. But they knew that anyway and, besides, I am not a fifteen-year-old orphaned Zambian girl living in a slum, totally responsible for the survival of her siblings. Who am I to judge?

The purchase of the additional drink had the desired effect. I was left on my own – mind you, I was the only person in the bar apart from the staff and the young girls. But not for long. In arrived a rather large, overweight, middle-aged *muzungu*. He didn't strike me as handsome or beautiful, but he was rich and so, I guess, he was instantly transformed into the opposite by the power of money. He greeted me with one of those knowing nods that recognised the presence of a fellow *muzungu* in a 'foreign land' with a common goal. He sat at the bar, ordered a drink and waited. Within a couple of minutes the young girls went over and sat around him. He flashed a few high denomination notes at the bar man, ordered a drink for 'his girls', entertained them with a few jokes or comments which they, as anticipated, feigned interest in. He then selected his 'chosen one'. She was young and attractive like the others and had caught his particular attention. He slipped his arm around her waist, she pretended to move away as if surprised and then placed her arm around his rather substantial midriff. The deal was done. He had his girl and the others moved away to await the next *muzungu* looking for their services. I finished my beer and moved towards the exit. My new 'friend' winked at me as he moved his hand towards the young African child's knee and said, 'Where would you get it, mate?' Then he winked again. I went out into the sun and fresh air, gave the drink to the security guard and went in search of Br John. But at that moment I really wished I could just jump onto a minibus, go back to the compound and feel clean again.

Chapter 9

Living with HIV/AIDS: People in Denial, People in Hiding

THIS ENCOUNTER WITH the young prostitutes in the bar is an experience that has stayed with me ever since. These young people, scarcely out of childhood, could have been our daughters, sisters, nieces or grandchildren had we not have been fortunate enough to be born in the affluent world. We can moralise all we want and point out that they have made their own choice, but it is easy to make moral judgements on others when you are free from the pressures that led them into prostitution. Like so many in the undeveloped world these girls are victims of poverty. I tried to picture the slum these girls came from as they put on their best clothes and make-up, as they prepared for another day (or night) seeking out the attentions of someone, anyone, with money. I tried to imagine the hovels these girls returned to and what awaited them there. Perhaps if we knew we would understand why they do what they do. Thinking about these young girls sets my mind racing back to a number of visits I have carried out with home-based care (HBC) teams in Africa. Home-based care teams are at the very front line in HIV/AIDS support in the slums and villages in sub-Saharan Africa. Home-based care workers, many of whom are volunteers, are trained lay workers who deliver anti-retroviral therapy (ART) to HIV-affected people in their homes. HBC teams also monitor them for drug side effects or disease progression and give adherence and counselling support. Invites to accompany a HBC team into a slum for people such as us are extremely rare and a privilege – they are also extremely difficult. On a home-based care visit you are allowed to accompany the volunteers in their everyday work as they go through the muddy lanes and open sewers of the township. They take you into the very depths of human suffering and misery to encounter some of the most marginalised, frightened and isolated people on this planet: those afflicted with HIV/AIDS. It is no exaggeration to say that those who have (or fear that they may have) HIV/AIDS are today's modern lepers. They are afflicted by a dreadful illness which, without access to anti-retrovirals (ARVs), will inevitably lead them to a horrific, painful, drawn-out and, generally, lonely death. They also face the likelihood that should their status become known they will be shunned, abandoned, feared and despised by neighbours, friends and even family. They live a silent and fearful life, uncertain of when the disease will visit them again, knowing that any recovery is only temporary and partial. They are an invisible people who suffer in silence and denial.

Hiding your status: dying alone – a lesson from Florencius

I have only met one person during all of my visits with HBC volunteers who admitted that he is HIV positive. Everyone else I encountered would willingly show me their TB clinic treatment card to demonstrate that they have 'only' tuberculosis. Not Florencius, whom I met while working with care workers in the Kibera slum in Nairobi.

Kibera is regarded as one of the biggest slums in Africa. You can actually smell Kibera from a long way off. One is struck by a certain sense of irony when one discovers that the slum takes its name from the Nubian word 'kibra', which means 'forest' or 'jungle'. It is a forest or jungle that one can smell on approaching the sea of mud-walled huts clustered so close together that you could walk for miles on top of them without touching the ground, if the corrugated roofs held your weight. Kibera is heavily polluted by soot, dust and other wastes. The slum looks as if it is built on trash, with waste, including excrement, filling the rough mud streets and streams, so only fetid pools remain. Small rubbish fires stutter on the roadsides, spreading acrid smoke near kiosks selling food. Pigs and goats forage in the waste and children play by filthy streams and drink from water pipes covered in garbage. Open sewage routes running only inches from the front doors and mud walls, in addition to the common method of excreta disposal – 'flying toilets' – contribute to contamination in the slum. The latter system of sewage disposal, though not unique to Kibera, is, according to the United Nations, 'the primary means of the primary mode of excreta disposal available to at least two-thirds of Kibera residents'.[25] (For the uninitiated and unsuspecting, a 'flying toilet' is a facetious name for the use of plastic bags for defecation, which are then thrown into ditches, on the roadside or simply as far away as possible). Piles of these polythene bags gather on roofs and attract flies. Some of them burst open upon impact and/or clog drainage systems. If they land on fractured water pipes, a drop in water pressure can cause the contents – both human and animal excreta – to be sucked into the water system. In the rainy season, drainage including excrement can enter residences. Children can often be seen swimming and playing in pools of stagnant waste. Such close contact leads to and increases diseases such as diarrhoea, skin disorders, typhoid, cholera and malaria. This is home to more than one million people – and one million people produce a lot of human waste.

It was in such dire surroundings that I met Florencius, a Kikuyan (or from the Agĩkũyũ people, as the Kikuyu prefer to be called) of approximately forty years of age, infected to the point of it being overwhelming. It was impossible *not* to know that he was HIV positive. He wore a bright blue tee shirt with the words '**HIV POSITIVE**' (in large, bold capital letters) across the front of it. It was also impossible to stop him from speaking about the fact that he was HIV positive and the need for others to come out and admit it. Much of my awareness about HIV/AIDS stigmatisation and the need to combat it came to me from people like Florencius. He had a saying, which he repeated like a mantra: 'If you remain silent you die'. He informed me that the denial of having HIV/AIDS occurs at a number of levels. Firstly, he informed me, the victims deny their HIV/AIDS status to themselves. There is the natural fear that to admit to yourself that you are HIV positive is to accept that the AIDS disease, with all its horrors, is your inexorable fate. Florencius then informed me that the second level of denial would involve not informing your family of your status, with the third level being denying it to your friends and neighbours. This is as a result of a fear of rejection, that all your friends will shun and abandon you, that your children will be taken away from you and that you will be driven out of your dwelling place. Guilt also accompanies this fear since often one's partner will have been infected (usually by the male partner). Mothers in particular are fearful about what will happen to their children when they are gone from this life. I have met many people during the home-based care visits who have either refused to go for a HIV test or return to the testing clinic to collect the results.

In my experience on HBC visitations, almost all parents who suffer from AIDS are not concerned for themselves; instead their concern is for the future welfare of their children. Florencius also informed me that not only is it important to combat the stigmatising of HIV/AIDS from a social and political point of view, it is also vital, he claimed, for the infected person him/herself, since by remaining in denial one effectively cuts oneself off from medicine, counselling services, proper diet and the other lifestyle factors that can combat the onset of the AIDS disease. Today Florencius is an AIDS counsellor and home-based care support worker who conducts AIDS awareness workshops in Kibera.

A HBC visit in Misisi

My wife, Philomena, and another of our volunteers, Daithi, had been invited by the home-based care team at the St Lawrence Centre to accompany its care volunteers on their home visitations. Philomena and Daithi set off with the home-based care workers shortly after ten in the morning. They were in good form, excited even, and looking forward to witnessing at first hand the work these volunteers carried out right in the middle of their community. They returned a little over three hours later completely emotionally exhausted and silent – perhaps traumatised. They needed their own space to reflect upon what they had just witnessed. The visitation in Misisi, which Philomena and Daithi had found so challenging and emotionally draining, had indeed been a difficult one. Brian, the leader of the home-based care team, had warned them of this beforehand but, like so much of life in the margins, nothing can properly prepare you for what you are about to encounter. When you enter a shack in a slum and your eyes get used to the dark, you become aware of the cramped conditions that is home to an entire family. You are also aware that the entire possessions of a family – accrued over a life-time – could fit into a couple of plastic bags. Coming from our 'throw-away' Western society, it is hard to imagine that people can have so little and live in such a confined space. You are also aware of the stench of the open sewers outside the front door, the noise and din of the nearby beer halls and the ever presence of abject poverty. And when your eyes become further adjusted to the dim light you notice the faint and quiet stirring from what you thought was an unmade bed. Slowly and deliberately the stirring takes on a distinctive human form, skeletal yet real. Carefully, and with ultimate dignity and modesty, this person manoeuvres him/herself to the side of the bed. The care workers introduce you to him/her and explain who you are and what you are doing in this most precious of places. You realise at once that you are in a sacred, private and privileged space – you have been invited into and have entered the home of one who is at the absolute

97

margins of human existence and endurance. The word 'forgotten' or 'abandoned' means nothing at all unless it is with these people. The word 'loved' might also be meaningless in this world of the margins were it not for the actions of those such as the home-based care workers, who enter this world in order to remind these victims of poverty and disease that they too are loved, that they too are special, that they too are God's children.

Atria: a child of God

In the West, some feel that HIV/AIDS is a moral issue and is a result of lifestyle choices for which the sufferer is, to a large degree, responsible. Tell that to a HIV positive child who became infected through a mother-to-child transmission; to a loving and faithful wife who contracted the virus from her infected (and unfaithful) husband; to the young orphaned girl who was forced into prostitution for survival; or to the young man who is in the final stages of the full-blown AIDS illness – an illness which he contracted because he was foolish enough to embrace the Western hedonistic culture, which has made everything a commodity, including the gift of sexuality. We are dealing with imperfect and flawed human beings here and, lest we forget the reality of HIV/AIDS, it might be worth considering the painful and humiliating death suffered by an AIDS victim. Michael Meegan gives us in the clearest, brutal, graphic and heart-rending terms a vivid description of the process of dying of AIDS and, in so doing, brings a humanity and dignity to the victim that is so often hidden behind the statistic. Atria, Meegan tells us, was a seventeen-year-old boy, at one time full of ambitions, dreams, plans and life. AIDS changed all that. In the developed stage of the disease, Atria goes through not only the unimaginable physical suffering of nausea, ulcers that make it impossible for him to eat or drink, muscle cramps where there is no muscle, diarrhoea, inflammation of his urinary tract, collapse of the buttocks and infection of the anus, blindness and pneumonia. According to Meegan, the greatest suffering which this young man has to endure is a sense of powerlessness and humiliation as his body disintegrates and, most of all, loneliness. The obscene death of an AIDS victim is described by Meegan as follows:

Atria is now in his last days of life. His tear ducts have dried up, his hair has fallen out, his bones are brittle. He has no muscle or fat and his heart is 70% weaker than pre-HIV. He has been eaten alive by repeated assaults on his body and has no resistance. All Atria's senses are shutting down. His skin is blistered and scaly as scabs cannot form. His finger and toenails have fallen out. The bedsores and ulcers have spread, becoming sources of multiple deep infections. Breathing is almost impossible and the slightest movement is slow and full of dreadful anxiety. I give him water drop by drop through a straw. I hold his frail stiffened hand, he is cold, he has no tears. I look into his eyes … I whisper to him and kiss him … He slowly inhales, half closes his eyes … He breathes out, very slowly … Atria's face relaxes, his tormented body loosens … he has gone. I held him in my arms and wept.[26]

In their darkness, HIV/AIDS victims such as Atria need and yearn for comfort and love, for affirmation of their humanity and the knowledge that their God-given dignity is not negated by an illness of which they are victim. Abandoned by all, on the brink of hopelessness and despair, they discover that they are not alone. The home-based care workers – many of them scarcely out of their youth – truly carry out a magnificent task of mercy, love and justice. 'To go to the margins and embrace the poor, the oppressed and forgotten' is a motto of immersion. To witness these courageous and dedicated volunteers seeking out HIV/AIDS victims and administering to their physical and spiritual needs is truly remarkable and the fullest living-out imaginable of this guiding principle. It was these remarkable people who taught me that HIV/AIDS is not a moral issue, but one of justice.

AIDS orphans: Africa's growing crisis

The last home the HBC group visited in Misisi was particularly disturbing. I have no doubt that HIV/AIDS care workers encounter this every day. It was more than simply a family of children who were about to lose the sole remaining parent and would have to look towards the extended family for support. This was a family about to become an 'orphan-led household', i.e. one in which the eldest sibling was to be given the responsibility of becoming the head of the household. In the affluent Western world, despite cuts in health and social services budgets, we would throw a raft of social services support at such a situation. And if these proved insufficient, we still have an extensive network of charities and other voluntary groups, which would be able to step in and lend much needed support. This is not so in Africa. Indeed, perhaps the greatest challenge to the social infrastructure of countries such as those in sub-Saharan Africa is yet to come, as the number of orphan-led households is set to soar. With the loss of the traditional breadwinners and the inability of the surviving grandparents to provide a long-term solution despite their heroic efforts, the extended family structure in countries such as Zambia is under enormous pressure. Africa's 'silent crisis' is described by Michael Fleshman in a United Nations Special Report, 'Protecting Africa's Children':

> To the tragedy of the 17 million people who have lost their lives to AIDS in Africa, add the 12 million orphaned children left behind. Traumatized by the death of parents, stigmatized through association with the disease and often thrown into desperate poverty by the loss of bread-winners, this growing army of orphans – defined as children who have lost one or both parents – is straining the traditional extended family and overwhelming national health and education systems in the most severely affected countries. The problem is particularly severe in Zambia, where, according to the US Agency for International Development (USAID), the number of orphans topped 1.2 million in 2000 – 1 in every 4 Zambian children.[27]

What we are facing here is the potential breakdown of a society due to the overwhelming scale of the AIDS pandemic. Such a crisis is beyond those even of refugees as a result of conflict, natural disaster or of famine. Fleshman points out that the needs of AIDS orphans are both immediate – for example, short-term survival – and extended. This includes access to education, guidance, care and training until the end of their adolescent years when they will, with proper support, be able to 'walk on their own'. In the same article, Stephen Lewis, UN special envoy for HIV/AIDS in Africa, describes the challenge facing all those involved with this human disaster:

> There has to be a Herculean effort made for these kids so we don't lose them. Otherwise you reap the whirlwind. You have a society where kids haven't been to school and therefore can't fulfil even basic jobs ... a society where a large proportion can have anti-social instincts because their lives will have been so hard. You have a generation of children who will be more vulnerable to exploitation and to disease because they won't have the same sense of self-worth.[28]

Already the scale of the crisis is beginning to reveal itself. In 2000, it was estimated that there were 540,000 orphans in Zambia as a result of AIDS. By 2005 this figure had risen to 710,000. Today it stands at 1.2 million with an expectation that within a few years it will have exceeded 1.5 million, out of a population of 10 million people. Add to that more than 75,000 street children and 150,000 disabled children, many of whom face abandonment, and you can see the growing crisis in Zambia and so many other countries in Africa.

'Within a few days this child will be a prostitute – can you blame her?'

It was little wonder when the home-based care workers saw this young girl that they recognised the seriousness of the situation. According to Philomena and Daithi, she was approximately thirteen or fourteen years of age, with beautiful shining eyes, plaited hair and a warmth that belied the life she had had and the one she was now facing. She should have been at school and preparing for a future filled with hope, promise and dreams. After all, is that not what all of us expect for ourselves and our children? However, she was not preparing for any sort of joyful and hope-filled tomorrow. Her mother had died earlier in the year and her father, in the final stages of AIDS, was being taken away to the John Hospice to die in care. One could not help but watch her anxious look and see the expressions of uncertainty, confusion, concern and fear in her eyes, the eyes of her young brother (aged approximately eleven or twelve) and a younger sister (approximately a year to two younger than the brother). The youngest child, a girl of around three years of age, played pitifully in the dusty lane outside the hovel, shielded from the enormity of what was happening by her age ... at least for now. Children grow up quickly in Misisi.

For the home-based care workers, the situation this young family was facing was particularly dire. Not only were the children at the point of becoming orphans, the care volunteers had identified that there was no extended family nearby that might be able to support them. Like many who have come from the villages into compounds such as Misisi in search of a better life, these children had only found even greater grinding poverty, squalor, misery and despair. Now, without the social network of the village, they had also found danger. Shock is too weak a word to describe the reaction of Philomena and Daithi when Brian, the senior home-based care worker, shook his head in sorrow and said, 'This is very serious. With no support this young girl will be a prostitute within days.' Then, after a pause, he muttered quietly, 'And who could blame her?' How many of us have a daughter, a sister or a niece of such an innocent and tender age who is faced with such an awful prospect? One day you are playing with your sister and her toys, helping to dress your younger brother, cooking for your sick father ... and the next you are forced into prostitution in order to feed your family.

That night Philomena and Daithi reported back what they had witnessed to the rest of the immersion volunteers. At times like that a feeling of powerlessness and hopelessness can sweep over you. You begin to question your effectiveness, your contribution and even your reason for being there. Do events such as those witnessed that day not make a mockery of everything that immersion is about? What good is it to say that you are for and with the marginalised and oppressed if you cannot save this one young girl from the nightmare of prostitution? Our instinct is to take her (and her remaining family) away from the horrors of the slum, but you cannot since for every person you might try to save there are hundreds of thousands of others in similar or even worse situations. Yet, if you cannot help the widow and the orphan, what is immersion about? Could it simply be a misguided and, ultimately, impossible attempt to help others in a situation way beyond our sphere of influence and means? Are we, despite our fine rhetoric and noble aspirations and ambitions, no different from the 'poverty tourists' who fly halfway

LIVING WITH HIV/AIDS: PEOPLE IN DENIAL, PEOPLE IN HIDING

around the world to 'drop into' a slum, take a few pictures and give the people there a few dollars and leave?

We are powerless – but only if we don't ask for help

Such silent thoughts were in everyone's head that night, I suspect. What could we, as a small group of immersion volunteers from Ireland, do in the face of such overwhelming sorrows and miseries? Then someone remembered the words of Peter Tembo, which he had first spoken to me on my initial visit to Misisi in 2002 and which subsequently had become a motto for Project Zambia: 'Remember, you cannot change the world; but together you can help us change our world'.

Those such as Peter Tembo, Angela Miyanda, John McCourt, Irene, Br Jacek, Brian, Peter McVerry and so many other energised people who are working tirelessly on behalf of the marginalised and forgotten victims of oppression, poverty and apathy, show us a way out of powerlessness and demonstrate that you cannot use the enormity of injustice and poverty in the world as an excuse for doing nothing. There is a phenomenal resource right there if you tap into it. We sat long into the evening reflecting on this message and discussing what we might be able to do to help in what appeared to be a seemingly impossible situation, yet one which we simply could not walk away from. We did not come up with any definite solution or concrete proposal, except one – the only sensible one which people in our situation could come up with. Accept what you can do, acknowledge what you can't and seek advice from those who have a wisdom way beyond your own.

It is interesting that often people from the West, who come to places that are so culturally and socially different from their home environment, feel that they have the solution to every problem. I'm not sure if it is as a result of Western rationality, which dictates that every problem must have a solution, or if it is simply some form of intellectual arrogance (which we, as inheritors of the Enlightenment, appear to possess in abundance). In either case, we miss the obvious and continue to blunder our way through people's sensitivities, cultures and lives. Fortunately, we recognised our own limitations. In other words, we hadn't a clue what, if anything, we could do in this case. So we decided to seek help from those who might know more than we did and the next morning met with Fr Oswald and Peter Tembo. We expressed all of our shared concerns about the fate of the young family and asked if there was anything we could do that might help. They asked us if we would be prepared to aid a project that would give long-term help to a number of orphan-led households. What is truly remarkable about these people is that they are always thinking about overcoming and resolving problems on a long-term basis. 'Sustainability' is their watchword, not short-term fixes. Something also striking about them is that they usually have the solution at hand. I suppose one shouldn't be surprised at this since, as they live with the problems on a daily basis, the solution is often clear to them. Perhaps the only thing that should surprise us is why we think that we have a solution that has escaped them. Fortunately, they were guiding us and not the other way round. When we agreed with their request, Fr Oswald and Peter took us to a piece of rather barren land in the corner of the St Lawrence Centre. It was a couple of acres in size with a few strips of land that were being used to grow vegetables and maize. Their dream was to have the whole area of land turned into an income-generating project for orphan-led households. 'Thirty-five separate plots of land feeding and supporting thirty-five little families. Three crops of maize a year and the same with tomatoes, lettuces, beans ...' We were trying to ask questions (as if we from Belfast had a clue about agriculture): 'What about irrigation? Where will they sell the produce? How will the children know when to plant the seeds? How much per plot?' We were entirely out of our league on this one. They were on fire. They were giving us the answers before we had even formulated the questions. Over the next hour we were taken on an amazing journey regarding how to turn a seemingly rock-hard piece of semi-concrete land into an oasis, which would provide food, income and security for these most vulnerable of people. So began the Irish Garden with its plots of irrigated and fertilised land, its orange plantation, chicken runs and piggery, a farm manager/instructor to ensure that the children learn how to grow the food for the market, and, of course, the farm tools and seeds. It is quite a hive of activity and a most, quite literally fruitful sign of our growing relationship with the people of the St Lawrence Centre. All we had to provide was a little bit of money – or, more accurately, convince people in Ireland to sponsor a plot of land for an orphan-led family. The cost for tools, irrigation and seeds? Thirty-five pounds sterling per plot.

In many ways, some of the more utopian aspects of the Gospels come to mind here, especially the Parable of the Mustard Seed. In the Gospel of Mark, Jesus instructs his disciples:

> The Kingdom of Heaven is like a mustard seed that
> someone took and sowed in his field; it is the smallest
> of all the seeds, but when it has grown it is the greatest
> of shrubs and becomes a tree, so that the birds of the
> air come and make nests in its branches.
>
> (Matthew 13:31)

At one level, such teaching can appear as simply allegorical: as expressing the belief that the kingdom (Church/community of believers) starts out small and becomes big. It can also be portrayed as thoroughly otherworldly, as belonging to the 'ever after' but certainly not to the 'here and now'. However, to portray such teachings as either allegorical (for example, as containing a simple but hidden meaning), otherworldly or even both is not only to miss entirely what Jesus was actually pointing towards, it also lends itself to a 'safe theology', which softens what is clearly an extremely radical 'here and now' worldly teaching and challenge. Far from being a passive teaching that urges the reader to wait for the kingdom to grow, this parable has revolutionary and praxical significance. It is utopian only in the sense that it points to another possible world order, a world order that begins with the smallest action but grows to be what is hitherto considered impossible. It also makes 'doing nothing' in the face of the scale of suffering and injustice not an option. Peter Tembo was right about 'helping us change our world'. Dreams can indeed become reality. All we have to do is allow ourselves to dream the impossible; the answers are already there.

Chapter 10

Jesus and the Marginalised

THE SENSE OF fear, isolation, loneliness and rejection experienced by people living in the margins was no doubt experienced by many of those whom Jesus encountered. Throughout the Gospels we are told not only that there were numerous groups of people who were marginalised by society and whose human dignity was not recognised – including lepers, women, sinners and the poor – but also that Jesus actively sought out these people and brought them back into the community. What is remarkable, indeed revolutionary, about the way Jesus approached those who were social outcasts is that he preferentially reached out to them. The idea of the 'preferential option for the poor' was a notion that exploded onto the radar of the Catholic Church in the latter decades of the twentieth century and continues to echo throughout the Church today. It was a phrase coined by the Peruvian Jesuit theologian Gustavo Gutierrez in 1967. It was adopted in 1968 at the Second General Conference of the Latin American Bishops (CELAM) in Medellín, Colombia, reaffirmed in Puebla in 1979 and has become a cornerstone of liberation theology right up to and including the present day. It is also important to note that this standpoint is not limited to the radical theologies that emanate from and have support in countries in the Developing World. As early as 1985, the Christian Brothers themselves viewed this idea as so important that they included it in their Constitution. Their Congregational Constitution states as follows:

> We are called to witness by prophetic action to our option for the poor and the oppressed, and to solidarity with them.[29]

Jesus was quite simple, direct and unequivocal in his preferential option for the poor, both in his teaching and in his practice. For Jesus, there was no avoidance or fudging of this question. He was absolutely, totally and unmoveably on the side of the poor and the socially excluded. If this set Jesus against the rich and powerful – those who excluded the marginalised and the oppressed in the first place – then so be it. And if this resulted in a conflict with the ruling authorities of the day, then the consequences were not to be avoided (and Jesus was unflinching in facing those consequences).

There are numerous examples in the Gospels of when Jesus came into direct conflict with those in authority: civic, political and religious. We often make the fundamental mistake in 'sanitising' Jesus, of making him the 'meek' and 'mild' Jesus who cured the lame, healed lepers, fed the five thousand, calmed the storm and so on. Of course he did those incredible things and was full of love and compassion, but Jesus was not simply a miracle worker and 'good teacher'. He was also the Son of God, who called God 'Abba' or 'Father' (John 16:25-33) and encouraged his disciples to do the same (Matthew 6:9-13). He never deviated from his mission: his

'Father's work'. By the end, Jesus proved impossible for the Jewish religious leaders (and for that matter the Roman authorities too) to deal with – other than by silencing him through putting him to death. After all, he had publicly befriended sinners and outsiders by eating with them (Mark 2:13-17; Luke 19:7), he forgave sinners (Mark 2:1-12), he defended his disciples when they broke Sabbath Law (Mark 2:23-28), he healed on the Sabbath (Luke 4:31-37), he publicly criticised and ridiculed the Jewish religious leaders (Mark 12:1-12; Luke 11:37-52) and condemned and physically opposed Temple worship (Luke 20:45-48). He confronted authority by standing resolutely on the side of the poor and the oppressed and told them that they were blessed (and not damned) and that '*theirs* was the Kingdom of Heaven' (Luke 6:17). The implication and corollary of this is that the Kingdom of God may not belong to the rich.

Peter McVerry disturbed my peace

It was the inspirational Jesuit priest and social activist, Peter McVerry, who instructed me in a new way of viewing and encountering Jesus and who unlocked my mind in approaching Jesus and the Gospels. Peter is one of these most annoying of people who, in the words of the writer Eamon Bredin, 'disturbs your peace'.[30] You can feel that you are content with life and that you have a handle on what makes you tick, your responsibilities and God … then you come into contact with people such as Peter McVerry. Peter started his ministry in Dublin in 1974 and has dedicated his life to combating the causes (as well as the effects) of poverty in Ireland. He is a radical social reformer who campaigns for a drastic re-distribution of the country's wealth and sees poverty as a scandal and a sin and regards fighting to eliminate it as a fundamental Christian duty. I have met Peter on numerous occasions, often in relation to immersion, and I come away from each experience both challenged and energised. The first time I met Peter was in 1997 when I was on a month-long retreat/reflection with the Christian Brothers and Presentation Order in the Emmaus Retreat Centre near Dublin. He had been invited to give a talk on the marginalised and poor. At that time I was very much in my 'doing and changing the world mode' and sat down expecting a revolutionary call-to-arms. I was certainly up for that. It didn't come – at least not in the way I had anticipated and hoped it would. Instead of being told what we must do for the poor – save *them* from oppression and poverty – we were asked to concentrate on what the poor can do to save us. Yes, we were given the Matthew 25 instruction/imperative about our duty towards those in need, and the magnificent passage from Isaiah 61:1-3 in which the prophet brings forth the good news of deliverance from oppression, poverty, injustice and brokenness. Indeed, it is of immense significance that Jesus commenced his public ministry with the reading of this remarkable passage in the synagogue at Nazareth:

> He unrolled the scroll and found the place where it was written, 'The Spirit of the Lord is upon me, because he has anointed me to bring good news to the poor. He has sent me to proclaim release to the captives and recovery of sight to the blind, to let the oppressed go free, to proclaim the year of the Lord's favour.'
>
> (Luke 5:17-19)

It is little wonder that when Jesus, having rolled up the scroll and looked around at the attentive audience of elders, scribes and devout Jews, said, 'Today this scripture has been fulfilled in your hearing' (Luke 4:21) there was outrage and demands that he be taken away and thrown off the top of the cliffs above Nazareth. And could you blame them? After all, this 'local boy' – 'Isn't he the son of Joseph?' (Luke 4:22) – had just announced the arrival of the Kingdom of God! I was entirely missing the point that Peter was making and falling into the same position of those who were in the business of rather seriously rejecting Jesus.

What 'disturbed my peace' and, thankfully, has stayed with me ever since was the seed that Peter McVerry planted in my head that day. If unswerving adherence to passages such as Matthew 25 and Isaiah 61 weren't sufficient for Christian response and action, then perhaps I was looking in the wrong direction. So I decided to approach Peter at an opportune moment after the session was finished. I didn't have to wait for long since Peter does stand about in the coffee area for as long as anyone wants to speak with him. It was no surprise to me that both of us were in agreement that God is not neutral. The God who we search for is one who is preferential towards the poor. All of the central tenets of the theology of liberation that I held to be true were confirmed by Peter. Yet Peter McVerry's teachings go beyond a simple acceptance or repeating of this radical approach to theology – or at least have pointed this hearer beyond a simplistic adherence to its categories. What is striking about his teaching is not just that God is a God for the poor; he is also a God of the poor. I was taken aback by this teaching, because in all my readings of the great liberation theologians, such as

Gustavo Guterriez, Leonardo Boff and José Sobrino, surely this distinction was precisely that which defined liberation theology and marked it off from some of the more conservative elements within the Church. Indeed, this was one of the primary teachings of the new theology. The Church must not simply be of the poor but for the poor. In *Jesus – Social Revolutionary?* Peter develops this idea in the most radical fashion and points out: 'Jesus announced a God who was not separated from God's people. Far from it, God was to be found there in the sick, the poor, the blind, the lame, the man robbed and beaten. God identified with the people. For Jesus, holiness consists not in separation from sinners but in proximity to sinners.'[31] This is a most dramatic and challenging teaching and one that altogether transforms our relationship with the poor and oppressed, as well as our image of God. The marginalised are not to be the object of our pity, viewed as poor unfortunate people to be helped or lifted up by charitable people and governments or even radical and revolutionary people of praxis. It is, in fact, in them that we find redemption and in them that we encounter God.

Let us recall once again Jesus' teachings on wealth in, for example, the story of the Rich Young Man. In the Gospel of Mark we are presented with a dramatic episode of immense importance and insight:

> As he was setting out on a journey, a man ran up, knelt down before him, and asked him, 'Good teacher, what must I do to inherit eternal life? Jesus answered him, 'Why do you call me good? No one is good but God alone. You know the commandments: You shall not kill; you shall not commit adultery; you shall not steal;

you shall not bear false witness; you shall not defraud; honour your father and your mother.' He replied and said to him, 'Teacher, all of these I have observed from my youth.' Jesus, looking at him, loved him and said to him, 'You are lacking in one thing. Go, sell what you have, and give to [the] poor and you will have treasure in heaven; then come, follow me.' At that statement his face fell, and he went away sad, for he had many possessions. Jesus looked around and said to his disciples, 'How hard it is for those who have wealth to enter the kingdom of God!' The disciples were amazed at his words. So Jesus again said to them in reply, 'Children, how hard it is to enter the kingdom of God! It is easier for a camel to pass through [the] eye of [a] needle than for one who is rich to enter the kingdom of God.'

(Mark 10:17-25)

It is little wonder that the disciples were stunned and shocked. After all, if a rich man who was obviously deemed to be in God's favour because of his riches[32] – and who has also kept God's Law since childhood – cannot be saved then who can? Certainly not the rag-tag bunch of fishermen, tax collectors, zealots, women, sinners, the sick, the marginalised, the oppressed and whoever else had responded to the invitation of the young rabbi from Nazareth to 'Come, follow me'. Yet it was precisely among these that Jesus centred his mission, his revolution.

Charity or Justice?

Poverty Tourism, 'Voluntourism' or Immersion?

Chapter 11

'Voluntourism': The Latest Western Fad to Hit Africa

OVER THE PAST decade, a new and increasingly popular form of social action has sprung up in the affluent world. Volunteer travel/volunteer vacations (generally referred to as 'voluntourism') combine both travel and volunteering for a charitable cause. In recent years, 'bite-sized' volunteer vacations have grown to such an extent that an entire industry has sprung up around it. The types of volunteer vacations are diverse, from low-skill work cleaning up local wildlife areas to providing high-skill medical aid in a foreign country. Volunteer vacation participants are diverse but typically share a desire to 'do something good' while also experiencing new places and challenges in locales they might not otherwise visit. Its supporters argue that voluntourism can make a difference, both in the communities where it occurs – through channelling money and other badly needed resources into impoverished communities – and in the individual traveller who receives the chance of a life-changing experience. However, it is not without its critics either. Lucy Ward, social affairs correspondent for *The Guardian*, explored this new phenomenon of voluntourism among gap-year students and cited VSO's, a leading charity, concern that this type of volunteering overseas might be damaging both for 'gappers' themselves and for the communities they work with.[33] According to Judith Brodie, director of VSO UK:

> While there are many good gap year providers, we are increasingly concerned about the number of badly planned and supported schemes that are spurious – ultimately benefiting no one apart from the travel companies that organise them. Young people want to make a difference through volunteering, but they would be better off travelling and experiencing different cultures, rather than wasting time on projects that have no impact and can leave a big hole in their wallet.[34]

Brodie concludes that these new voluntourists may become the 'new colonialists', with the benefits of such ventures tending to be on the side of the traveller who takes on the role of the 'do-gooder', imposing his/her solutions on poor communities. Furthermore, there is a danger that much of the money is spent on maintaining the voluntourism agency or wasted on highly questionable projects, and that this phenomenon simply reinforces the stereotype (both in the undeveloped world and in the affluent world) that those in the margins are helpless victims of poverty who are incapable of solving their own problems. '*They* are the problem, *we* are the solution' would appear to shape the mindset of some of the organisations that engage in such activities.

It would be wrong, however, to place all voluntary organisations who are working in the margins – both locally and globally – in this bracket. There are numerous examples of excellent practice and inspirational vision. Local charities, such as St Vincent de Paul, and world-wide justice organisations, such as Concern and Trócaire, exemplify the selfless and courageous sense of service that lie at the heart of Christian discipleship. Furthermore, many people who volunteer with organisations that may be open to the above criticisms are motivated by the highest of ideals and principles. At the same time, however, some of the criticisms of badly guided volunteering may have some validity.

Some questionable examples

It can be safely said that in all walks of life and in all places we encounter situations that shock us. It is no different in Africa. I suppose as an immersion volunteer it is all too easy to be over critical about how other volunteering organisations or projects operate. It is also generally unfair since, quite often, we only get a 'snap shot' of what another group is trying to do. Sometimes, however, you do come across things that are simply not right. A couple of years ago we met one American woman in Zambia who had just spent $30,000 on sanctuaries for orphaned monkeys. 'They were so cute, I just fell in love with them!' she told us. I know that it was her money and that she was entitled to do with it whatever she wanted, but with orphanages for Zambian children in every small town and with a generation of grandparents toiling everyday to provide food for their grandchildren … I couldn't comprehend this.

Around the same time we met a group of twenty sports studies students from universities and colleges throughout

England. They had received a grant to spend a month in Africa teaching the children to play team games such as football, netball, rounders, and so on. We pointed out to one of the students that all of the children knew how to play such games, to which the student (with two days' experience in Africa) suggested that this could not be the case since so many of them just seemed to be sitting around doing nothing. We had to inform her that since most of the children receive only one meal each day, usually a cup of maize porridge when they come to school, perhaps they didn't feel in much form of running around.

Perhaps one of the most current and relevant issues concerning volunteering at this time is the issue of the building of homes, wells, schools and other facilities in the shanty towns, slums and villages in the Third World. Projects of a construction nature attract support and question in equal measure. For some, such projects are self-evidently of value. The need for living, health, educational and sanitary facilities is so glaringly obvious that only the most cynical, suspicious and uncaring of people could object to any group or organisation that engages in such work. And such an approach to seeking to 'make a difference' is very popular. Indeed, there are numerous organisations and agencies throughout the affluent countries who advertise opportunities to engage in such activities. And, no doubt, many do indeed make a real difference to a considerable number of people and communities in the margins. Nevertheless, at the same time there are a number of valid questions that need to be addressed by some of the organisations engaged in this type of action.

- **Outcomes:** Does the 'final product' – be it the construction of a house, well or school – justify the considerable expenditure, such as travel and other costs, associated with the particular project? This is an entirely valid and important question to consider as it does go to the heart of the volunteering issue: what is the primary purpose of the project? Does it deliver value for money? Does it (inadvertently) deprive local workers (and their families) of an income? Does it empower the host community?

- **Ownership and Allocation:** This is an extremely important issue that defines the value and integrity of the project. It is not a media-driven fabrication where some people, who had been allocated homes built by volunteers from the affluent world, have moved out of their houses into shacks so that they could rent them out for huge profit. Every missionary I have met in Africa could take you to some project nearby his/her mission station that is a testimony to such corruption. I myself have witnessed numerous examples of ownership being in the hands of corrupt elements. Projects include housing, access to education, income-generation, orphanages and even access to toilets!

- **The Experience:** What people who go on a volunteering project do and experience while they are in the undeveloped world is of significance. Some, indeed, many projects involve enculturation, developing bonds of solidarity and mutual affirmation, and establish structures that will aid long-term relationships and sustainability. Sometimes, inevitably, some people may simply 'park' the experience in their 'life CV' and move on. There also arises the question concerning the balance between the volunteering and tourism aspects. Many voluntourism websites and associated travel agencies are quite open about offering the opportunity to combine both the volunteering aspect and the tourism element. There is, of course, nothing wrong with this per se, however, it could be suggested that for some the motivation in volunteering in the first place is not completely other-directed or altruistic.

All of these questions can – and should – be asked of groups and organisations such as the Christian Brothers' Developing World Immersion Programme, Trócaire, Concern and others who see themselves most certainly not in terms of being tourists, but rather as people motivated by an altogether world vision based on justice. So, what makes immersion/justice oriented groups and movements different from voluntourism?

Deus caritas est: beyond good work to God's work?

In the Encyclical *Deus caritas est*, Pope Benedict XVI stressed the fundamental importance of the 'formation of the heart' in placing oneself at the service of others.[35] This apparently unthreatening and gentle phrase is of a much more radical and challenging nature than it may seem. In dealing specifically with helping those in need, Pope Benedict points out that professional competence is, naturally, important. It is not enough, however. Because we are dealing with people – and marginalised people at that – competence alone is not sufficient. According to Benedict, 'Human beings always need something more than technically proper care. They need humanity. They need heartfelt concern.'[36] Pope Benedict then goes on to identify what makes the Christian vision and practice of 'caritas' different from a secular model of charity. It is not simply about meeting the immediate or even long-term needs of people in the margins. True Christian 'caritas' involves and is motivated by a deep love for and identification with the other. According to Pope Benedict:

> They [caritas volunteers] need to be led to that encounter with God in Christ which awakens their love and opens their spirits to others. As a result, love of neighbour will no longer be for them a commandment imposed, so to speak, from without, but a consequence deriving from their faith, a faith which becomes active through love (cf. Gal 5:6).[37]

It is not simply that this motivation of faith gives 'added value' or 'increased outcome' to the struggle against poverty. It makes it a completely different activity altogether.[38] The affirmation of (and immersion with) the human person becomes the centre of the endeavour and not simply the objective outcome; justice replaces charity.

Immersion as a 'formation of the heart'

I believe that there are two fundamental principles that set immersion aside from a purely charity-driven approach to combating poverty. The first is an awareness that at the heart of immersion lies an identification with the other. For immersion volunteers the poor and oppressed are not seen as outside objects of our compassion; rather, they are part of us and we are part of them. We are one people and one community. The separation between the two agents in immersion – the host communities on the one hand and the immersion groups who are invited into that sacred space – is abolished in this coming together, this unity in which we become one, which is demanded by justice. By going to work in solidarity with those in the margins we are not doing anything extraordinary or heroic. We are simply doing what is right, what is just.

What also distinguishes the immersion process from some of the purely charity-focused groups is this: on return from the Developing World, many people from some of these voluntourist organisations slot back into society and return to play their part in the service of global capitalism without questioning the way in which our affluent world and choices are linked to the conditions they have just left. Some may even hold senior positions in global corporations that create and perpetuate the very conditions that these charity agencies are seeking to eliminate. A major difference now, however, is that the returning volunteer – as distinct from the pure voluntourist – can no longer claim that he/she is unaware of what is happening in the margins. Poverty and its causes can no longer be denied. The defence made by some who lived in Nazi-occupied Europe during the Second World War in relation to the Holocaust – that they did not know what was happening – cannot be used by any of those who have directly witnessed the scandalous conditions so many millions of our fellow men, women and children are forced to endure. The unavoidable simple question must be addressed by every returning volunteer:

'So, now you know, what now?' We, as individuals, are not responsible for the injustice that our world is. We are, however, aware of how unjust a place the world is and this new consciousness demands action.

Plato's Allegory of the Cave, or 'entering the Matrix'

In Book VII of his famous work, *The Republic*,[39] Plato invites us to imagine a dark, subterranean prison in which humans, from infancy, are bound by their necks and restricted to a single place. Elaborate steps are taken by unseen forces to supply and manipulate the content of the prisoners' visual experience. The prisoners are chained in such a way that all they can see are shadows thrown on a wall in front of them. All they know of life are these shadows. They think that these shadows are reality and, having known nothing else than this world of illusion and shadows, they are satisfied to live their lives in this way. After all, this is the only world they know, the only world that can conceivably exist. Furthermore, the cumulative effects of this imprisonment are so thorough that, if freed, the prisoners would be virtually helpless. They would be so conditioned and shaped by their experience that, even if exposed to the truth, they would refuse to accept this. They would wish to remain imprisoned even after their minds grasped the horror of their condition. Plato goes on to invite us to consider that a prisoner does indeed escape and comes to understand the relationship between the prison and the world outside, between illusion and truth. After a difficult and painful struggle (initially blinded by the sunlight and wanting to return to the 'safety' of the cave), he would come to see things as they are and realise how limited his vision was in the cave. He would come to understand those representations or shadows in the cave to be imperfect, like pale copies of the full reality now grasped in the mind. He would not wish to swap the newly discovered truth of the 'real world' with the false and pale illusions of the cave. Yet, he is a philosopher, one who loves wisdom, and he has a duty to free all others from ignorance and slavery. He would be quite unwilling to return. Yet if he returned to the cave, the freed prisoner would be the object of ridicule, disbelief and hostility. The captives would conclude that he had gone mad, that his mental state was proof enough to remain in the cave and that the former prisoner who was now attempting to remove their chains and lead them out of the cave was deserving of death.

The 1999 film *The Matrix* contains many similarities and parallels to Plato's parable on ignorance and knowledge. Like the prisoners of the cave, the people trapped in the Matrix only see what the machines want them to see. They are tricked into believing that what they experience in the Matrix is the true reality that exists. Like the captive who escapes from Plato's cave, Neo, the protagonist in *The Matrix*, discovers that what he has been presented with his entire life is only a reflection, or merely shadows and distortions of the truth. The *real* truth is the very opposite of that generated and maintained in the Matrix. The inhuman reality of the Matrix is hidden from those who actually experience it.[40]

This, in fact, is the condition of much of humankind today. Many people live in a world of ignorance, shadow and denial. Many are even comfortable with this ignorance since it is all that they know. Immersion, however, helps us to see the world as it is. It challenges us to change this inhuman world. It forces us to stare into the faces of those who have been deliberately abandoned and condemned by an uncaring system that views everyone and everything as mere instruments to be exploited and used in order to increase and pay homage to the only God it recognises: profit. Immersion forces us to look into the mirror that reflects ourselves and liberates us from the false images, which greed, selfishness and materialism has constructed. We cannot go back to the cave or 're-plug' ourselves back into the Matrix. The immersion experience is not limited to time spent on an immersion site, or time and energy spent afterwards working on behalf of the community entered while on immersion. Immersion is a journey, a transformation through which our very being, world-vision and totality of relationships are radically altered. We must carry that journey – that seed that was planted in the margins – into our lives back at home. In Ireland today, the travelling community, the homeless, drug abusers and others who are socially excluded are no less victims of structural injustice and neglect than those suffering from the effects of famine and other victims of poverty in the Developing World. They all share one thing in common: they do not matter. They are not important enough to matter. Do we truly affirm the human dignity of those at the margins, demand justice and show true solidarity with those who are suffering? Or do we utter pious words and supplications safe from daring to be a disciple? Do we act as 'charity voluntourists' for two weeks in some far-off country, thousands of miles away, or do we take on the mantel of justice into every aspect of our lives?

Chapter 12

A Brief Encounter with Some of the Boys

I MET FOUR lads in the hostel I was staying in in Lusaka. Their accents were genuinely Irish and they were in good form. It was Friday night and they were catching the Saturday morning flight back to London and then connecting to Dublin. They were having a couple of beers and why not? They didn't look the tourist types – no designer sunglasses or tee shirts announcing that they had been on safaris in Kenya, white water rafting down the Zambezi or bungee jumping at Victoria Falls. No, they didn't look that sort. They seemed to be ordinary guys, so I decided to join them. I found out that they had been working up north in the Copper Belt for a month on a building project with one of the religious orders. We talked of the coming Gaelic football and hurling season, the current state of the Irish soccer team and many other bits and pieces that connect you with home. We got round to talking about what the lads had been doing over the past month and what they thought of Africa and how it had changed them.

'Changed' perhaps was the wrong word. 'Builders all, we are', they told me, 'and, by Christ, we did some block-laying up there.' This grabbed my imagination. As a teacher who is absolutely useless and entirely disinterested in DIY at home, but who is also a late (and poor) convert to the construction game via immersion, I found myself seeking advice from these genuine experts from Ireland on how to build during the rainy season, how many tiers high you could build per day with the quality of block that is made in Zambia, the relative merits of the purchase of a cement mixer for major building projects versus the employment of local labour, and so on.

After my attempts to grasp some of the rudiments of how to successfully build in Zambia, we set about discussing the other aspects of their time in Africa. 'Where did you stay?' I asked them. I expected that they would give me a name of a basic backpackers' hostel or the religious order they were working with or some other local arrangement. There was a few seconds of embarrassed silence and muted laughter. Then the more vocal member of the group muttered that they had stayed initially in the community house with the religious order and then moved on to stay in a small hotel in the town. 'What happened with the community house?' I wondered. I have stayed often enough with missionary orders in Africa to know that they will accommodate anyone and anything if at all possible and reasonable. They are great places to stay in. At one level, you are immediately welcomed as part of a community which is working both for and with the poor. At the same time, the design of the mission houses today enables you to have your own private space for sleeping and reflection. Alongside the communal living areas such as a lounge, kitchen, dining room and so on, the religious houses tend to have private sleeping accommodation, often with your own bathroom. Sometimes there will be a separate volunteer house for those who are working alongside the religious orders or who are simply passing through. The various orders with whom I have stayed in Africa are exceptionally attentive to the needs of volunteers, so I found it strange that these lads from Ireland had moved out of their original accommodation. I wondered if the religious community had had a problem with electricity, water or some other essential facility that necessitated their moving on to new surroundings. 'Not a bit of it', I was told, 'We were asked politely to leave.' Well, that certainly perplexed me. 'Why?' I asked. The boys all swore blind that they hadn't done anything wrong; it was just that the missionaries had an issue with the boys traipsing back from the beer hall in the early hours of the morning and bringing with them some of the local African lads looking for a party and African girls looking for 'business'. 'But we didn't do anything wrong and it was mighty *craic*. And besides, sure we never missed a day's work.'

Rarely am I rendered utterly speechless, but I certainly was on that occasion. I fumbled for words to point out the rather obvious. Didn't they realise that their behaviour was putting the religious community in a seriously compromised and, indeed, impossible position? Surely they understood that the integrity and reputation of the missionaries, the relationship and trust they had built with the people over decades, the actual projects themselves, all of these were being undermined by their selfish and questionable moral and social behaviour? Could they not appreciate the legacy they would leave behind by this sort of behaviour? Did they not care?

Without trying to be controversial or critical, I suggested to my new friends that it appeared to me that they were operating out of two completely contradictory and opposing visions of life.[41] On the one hand, they see themselves as working in solidarity and justice with the marginalised and oppressed – at least up to the end of the working day. On the other hand (after the end of their building activities), they were using the very same people as means to their own ends. They appeared to be quite aware of everything they were doing yet saw no contradiction. 'Look, Aidan, we know what you're saying, but we came here to build this workshop and we did. Now, how we get on after we finish work is up to us. We did our bit and we did a grand job.' On that we parted company. I wished them a safe journey home and we shook hands. One of them suggested that perhaps I might visit them when they return to Africa. 'We'll be back next year, Aidan. If you're about you can come up and stay with us. It'll be mighty *craic*. You'd love it.' Somehow I thought this was an invitation I might not be taking up.

But we're better than that, aren't we?
We all like to think of ourselves as well-balanced, holistic people who are motivated by a sense of justice and love for our fellow human beings. We are decent people who would never condone, never mind commit an act of exploitation or harm to any other human being. We are on the side of justice, aren't we? When we watch the news of tragic events such as the war in Iraq, the plight of the Palestinians, the suffering of victims of famine, disease or natural disaster, we often express, or at least feel a sense of empathy, pity and compassion. How often have we uttered the words 'God help those poor people' when witnessing such scenes on our television screens or while talking with work colleagues or friends over a cup of coffee? Sometimes we go further, especially, for example, when we

see images of the countless victims of war, ethnic cleansing, torture and barbarism, and start to advocate simplistic solutions that usually involve some brutal direct action, which the holder of the opinion often states that he/she would have no hesitation in doing him/herself. And when we see people suffering from hunger, poverty, child labour or HIV/AIDS, don't we often hear people – and ourselves – say that all of us should be prepared to do whatever it takes to help these people? Then, the next day, we find many of us buying clothes made by bonded child labour in India or China, or bananas or coffee from what are still effectively slave plantations in Latin America. We disapprove of exploitation but to end it would come at a price ... to us in the West. Do we really love our neighbour or do we even love our neighbour enough to allow this love to impact upon our lives? I suppose it depends on what we mean by 'love'.

The fundamental human characteristic of *agape* – of true, other-directed love and identity with the other – has, to a large extent, been lost, or at least very severely limited in our individualistic, materialistic Western culture. Matthew Fforde points out in his most recent work on 'desocialised society' that our consumerist society minimises genuine human contact and produces a form of isolated, individual living largely cut off from one's fellow men and women.[42] The Thomist idea that each person is in reality God's reflection or the Marxian notion of a 'species-being' (*Gattungswesen*) who can only realise his/her true self and individuality in and through genuine human relationships with his/her fellow person, is alien and in opposition to a social order in which everyone else is regarded as a potentially hostile and foreign other.[43] The dynamic of our modern materialist world is a matrix of materialist visions of humanity (including relativism) that seek to deny the existence of the soul, generate a lifestyle of selfish individualism and cause a breakdown in community. Every aspect of our inner life, every trace of our real sensuous humanity, is undermined by a world outlook that regards people as 'things' or objects that have no intrinsic value and, at best, are there to be used or manipulated to achieve one's own selfish goals. Worse still, this fragmentation of human living is imported into each human subject. In our materialist consumer society, we are forced to adopt different ways of viewing and relating to our fellow men and women. On the one hand, with our friends and family we are expected to strive to be loving, caring and other-directed. In all other aspects of life, however, we must act in accordance with the prevailing social and economic order: as if our fellow men and women are not our brothers and sisters, but rather are to be regarded as outsiders, as strangers of no intrinsic value. Pope John Paul II pointed out, however, that such thinking, based on unbridled selfishness and individualism, is completely at odds with the Christian vision of humanity.[44] The Christian answer to Cain's question (Genesis 4:9), 'Am I my brother's keeper?' must be a resounding 'yes'. Solidarity or Christian love is not to be reserved only for certain people or relationships. It is to be universalised as it is an integral part of the Church's salvific mission and is based on – and reflective of – the Christian understanding of the goal of humanity and the nature of God. According to Pope John Paul:

> Beyond human and natural bonds, already so close and strong, there is discerned in the light of faith a new model of the unity of the human race, which

must ultimately inspire solidarity. This supreme model of unity, which is the reflection of the intimate life of God, one God in three Persons, is what we Christians mean by the word communion.[45]

Unfortunately, in a world dominated by materialism and individualism, other forces seek to disrupt this 'new model' of unity and solidarity. Other forces are playing a role in our lives as well. We are not immune.

Dr Jekyll and Mr Hyde

The myth of the werewolf and the story of Dr Jekyll and Mr Hyde symbolise perfectly the condition of people in modern consumerist society, as many of us continually find ourselves being pressurised by the conflicting demands of being human, living for others and living for oneself. The privatisation and compartmentalisation of morality, values and conscience present an enormous challenge to all who seek a unity of self and others and who strive to live their lives in accordance with justice. Each human person is forced to live his/her life according to the conflicting and mutually hostile demands of the competing rationalities of modern living. We live in a culture dominated by an inability to arrive at any rationally justifiable agreement on the nature of humankind, society, truth or justice. In such an uncertain relativist world, we often operate according to completely differing and contradictory sets of norms and rules, what the philosopher Alasdair MacIntyre calls 'competing rationalities'.[46]

It is not simply the 'private individual/public citizen' dichotomy or the sociological categories of *Gemeinschaft* and *Gesellschaft*[47] that confront man in the postmodern social world of the twenty-first century. The human condition for modern Western man today is much more fragmented and torn apart than at any other time in human history. We do not have any unified vision, world map or connection with or knowledge of ourselves, never mind with or of anyone else. Therefore, before we engage or interact with someone, we have to work out which type of relationship or engagement this encounter is. Is it social, personal, economic, philosophical, professional, spiritual or some other category that is making up our fragmented lives? Which rulebook are we using? We are to be Socratic in our quest for truth, like Jesus in our relationships with others, Kantian in our approach to ethics, Hobbesian in how we approach the 'real world', Machiavellian in the sphere of politics, Keynesian in the economic world and, as well as this, whatever private guru we have selected in those other personal spheres of our social/personal lives that do not fit into any of the realms above. It is no wonder that modern human living is such a confused and contradictory task.

Nowhere is this confusion and contradiction more evident than when we go from listening to the words of the Gospel or participating in the Eucharist at Mass back into the 'real world'. Jesus' teachings are simple – in the sense of being unambiguous and clear – and challenging without compromise. Unlike the Jewish religious authorities and experts of his day, who had managed to produce from the Ten Commandments a plethora of rules and regulations that effectively strangled the spirit of the relationship between God and his people, which the Commandments underpinned, and reduce it to one of strict external obedience, Jesus sought to restore the spirit to the centre of Jewish religious and social life. In the story of the Greatest Commandment (Mark 12:28-34), we are treated to the way in which Jesus saw humanity, God and the world. We are told that a teacher of the Law came up to Jesus and asked him, 'Which commandment is the most important of all?' Undoubtedly the Jewish religious experts, upholders and, indeed, guardians of the law had endless disputes and discourses on which rule was most important and how the law was to be properly adhered to. Observance to detail and duty were of the utmost importance. Yet Jesus' answer completely ignores such teachings and ritualised practices. Jesus replied:

> Listen, Israel! The Lord our God is the only Lord. Love the Lord your God with all your heart, with all your soul, with all your mind, and with all your strength. The second most important commandment is this: Love your neighbour as yourself. There is no other commandment more important than these two.
>
> (Mark 12:29-31)

Mark informs us that in response to this the teacher of the law concurs with Jesus and adds, 'It is more important to obey these two commandments than to offer animals and other sacrifices to God' (Mark 12:33). The comment is of considerable significance because animal and other offerings (mostly money) had become the standard and most important form of religious practice associated with Temple worship in Jerusalem and was the basis of the Jewish religion itself. We are told by Mark that Jesus noted his reply and said, 'You are not far from the Kingdom of God' (Mark 12:34).

Those who take this story to mean that Jesus simplified the over-complicated and rule-dominated religion of the Jews by suggesting that everything in the Torah could be covered by returning to the Ten Commandments, and further reducing them to only two, 'love God, love your neighbour', entirely miss the point. Jesus was not merely pointing out that the 'love God' command was sufficient to cover the first four commandments, or that if you 'love your neighbour as yourself' you would automatically keep the following six commandments, such as not killing, stealing or bearing false witness. Of course, these are the outworkings of loving God and loving your neighbour; however, for Jesus there is much more to this teaching and way of being than the list of imperatives and/or prohibitions contained in the Ten Commandments or, indeed, the Torah. In the passage of the Greatest Commandment, Jesus stresses the unity of loving God, loving one's neighbour and the creation/coming of the kingdom. Far from giving us a simplistic teaching with a completed answer, Jesus presents us with a profoundly rich teaching and poses an unfinished set of questions and challenges. By inextricably linking love of God and love of one's neighbour, and by stating that these are the conditions for the kingdom, Jesus refutes any bifurcation of human action. To truly love God necessitates a real and concrete love of one's neighbour. And how does one love one's neighbour? Jesus' teachings on this certainly do not need unpacking or interpretation. Again and again, through his teachings and actions, Jesus instructs us that we can only love God through loving our neighbour and we do this by reaching out and affirming the dignity of those who have been abandoned or rejected by 'respectable society'.

Peter McVerry points out that living the Gospel involves recognising each person as a reflection of God. According to McVerry, 'When Jesus comes and finds someone whose dignity as a human being, as a child of God, was being undermined or denied by the attitudes of society and the way in which they are treated, then he must respond.'[48] The episode that McVerry selects to illustrate Jesus' response to the denial of dignity and marginalisation of those not deemed 'in observance to the Law' – in other words 'respectable' – is taken from the Gospel of Luke when Jesus visited the home of Simon the Pharisee:

> A Pharisee invited him to dine with him, and he entered the Pharisee's house and reclined at table. Now there was a sinful woman in the city who learned that he was at table in the house of the Pharisee. Bringing an alabaster flask of ointment, she stood behind him at his feet weeping and began to bathe his feet with her tears. Then she wiped them with her hair, kissed them, and anointed them with the ointment. When the Pharisee who had invited him saw this he said to himself, 'If this man were a prophet, he would know who and what sort of woman this is who is touching him, that she is a sinner.'
>
> (Luke 7:36-40)

What is of essence here is that this woman, a prostitute, was clearly outside the law and, therefore, outside of society. *She* had put herself outside of society because of *her* actions. Yet Jesus responded to her, despite her social status, by affirming her dignity and bringing her back into the community. By so doing he challenged the attitudes of society itself and, as McVerry points out, so too did Jesus become marginalised by society:

> The challenge that Jesus posed by eating with sinners lay in the simple, but deeply profound, act of looking at a human being whom society considered of little value, of little use, of little worth and recognising that person's extraordinary dignity as a child of God – indeed, as we shall see, recognising their privileged place in the mind and heart of God. That simple, God-like act of reaching out and caring for someone whom most people considered of no value reflected God's vision of humanity and the compassion of God. In reaching out to them, Jesus revealed the nature of God, and, in doing so, fulfilled the mission that God had given to him.[49]

For Jesus, those whose dignity is denied are denied justice. Jesus' condemnation of those who deny justice to the marginalised and oppressed – who are the very people who create the conditions that make and keep these people marginalised and oppressed – echoes that of the prophet Isaiah when he condemned (in more sense than one) the rich and powerful:

> You are doomed! You make unjust laws that oppress my people. That is how you prevent the poor from having their rights and from getting justice. That is how you take the property that belongs to the widows and orphans.
>
> (Isaiah 10:1-2)

In our contradictory and split lives we do not see that the denial of dignity is a denial of justice. We respond to the victims of poverty in much the same way as the Pharisees responded to Jesus – but in a more confused way. At least the Pharisees used a single rule to measure human behaviour: rigorous adherence and unquestioning observance to the law. To go outside of the law was to go to the margins. Our fragmented world vision ensures that we actually have no unified response, even within ourselves, in respect to the marginalised. I can go to Mass on Sunday, pray for the poor and give alms to the Saint Vincent de Paul on the way out of Holy Family Church. I can support the work of Trócaire and put a collection box in my home at Lent, purchase fair trade coffee at the Third World stall and even sign a petition against Third World debt. But if that is all that I do, is there not a danger that I am failing to address or even ask more fundamental questions: 'Why does such poverty exist? Why is it allowed to exist?'

It was the great champion of the poor of Brazil, Dom Helder Camara, Archbishop of Recife and Olinda, who famously said, 'When I give money to the poor they call me a saint. When I ask why are they poor they call me a communist.' In this brief and, apparently, simple sentence, Archbishop Camara demonstrated in the clearest and most concise form the difference between charity and justice. The purely charity model – giving without demanding justice – allows us to give without changing either the structures that create and perpetuate poverty and oppression or ourselves and our own personal lifestyles. Without asking the question, 'Why are they the poor?' nothing of substance is changed. The poor remain outside of me and my life: in the margins. It is possible that after fulfilling my duty on a Sunday morning I can resume my life as a self-interested individual, who engages in the exploitation of my fellow man through my work, my social relationships, my personal interests or through my silence and acceptance of the injustices that permeate our world. Thus, in the moral sphere, we are told to 'love our neighbour' while simultaneously being urged to do precisely the opposite in so many other aspects of life.

We encounter much of this bi-polarity of consciousness all the time. It is part of modern living. We are continually bombarded with advertisements to encourage consumerism and greed, which create poverty and marginalisation; then comes an advertisement or news item encouraging people to support marginalised and poor people. I have no doubt that in the US Army bases in Iraq there are collection tins for children wounded and maimed in the conflict there. And, no doubt, some of those who that day have flown bombing raids over villages in Iraq or have created 'collateral damage' – the taking of innocent human lives – will put money into those collection jars. Ali Abbas, the (then) twelve-year-old child from Iraq, who lost both his arms as well as both his parents and fourteen other relatives in a coalition missile attack on their farm near Baghdad in March 2003, is a most interesting case in point. The entire world media certainly jumped on this story, but not from any perspective of justice. Instead of asking a rather obvious question such as, 'Why was this child deliberately mutilated in this way and so many of his family members blown to pieces?' the media focused on the 'human interest' dimension. The media avidly followed his progress through his initial treatment in Kuwait and his subsequent 'rehabilitation' in Britain where, the media was delighted to tell us, he had been receiving free tuition at a school in London. Somewhere in all of this the truth has been lost as one marginalised and brutalised child becomes a victim once again – this time of political interests and the cynical manipulation of public opinion by the media.

We should not be too complacent in believing that such confused thinking only occurs in others. It is, in fact, a condition of the modern Western world vision, one which also presents a massive challenge to all of us. Clearly two (or more) completely opposing and contradictory world visions compete within each of us as we strive to 'do the right thing'. We are urged, encouraged and, indeed, even commanded to stand on the side of the poor and to oppose injustice and oppression. Yet, the very values and economic and political conditions that make these people poor are precisely those that we, in the affluent Western world, are urged to embrace. It is no wonder that the builder boys I met in Zambia lived a paradoxical and confused life when they came to Africa. After all, surely all they had done was bring their bifurcated and fragmented life vision from Ireland to Africa and live it there?

Temple worship and Jesus

Just when I was getting quite comfortable reflecting on the short fallings of all of those who live their lives according to so many contradictory rules and world visions, I picked up Peter McVerry's work again and started to read the chapter entitled 'Where is God to be Found?'[50] For those who are satisfied with a perception of Church based solely on an institutional vision, with its accompanying levels of hierarchy, a strict adherence to rules, regulations and practices, and a marked emphasis on 'finding God' in the private spaces of a church building, this chapter makes challenging reading. McVerry outlines in the clearest terms Jesus' rejection of the Temple worship that dominated Jewish thinking and practice at that time. To seek God in the Temple was to seek God away from people. It was not only to look in the *wrong* place, it was, in fact, to look for a *wrong* God. According to McVerry, the notion of 'holiness' and separation from all that was 'unholy' (for example, the poor, the marginalised, outsiders and sinners) in the Jewish religion led to a form of worship of an all-holy God who was remote from and entirely distinct and separated from His people. God could only be worshipped in the Temple – since that is the only place He was. The priests controlled that worship and, in so doing, controlled access to God. However, McVerry points out that, for Jesus, this is precisely where God *cannot* be found. His actions described by Mark (11:15-16) in turning over the tables of the buyers and sellers and driving them out of the Temple, and his condemnation that 'my Father's house is a house of prayer for the people of all nations, but you have turned it into a den of robbers' (11:17), is a clear disassociation from the religious practices of Temple worship and the unjust power structures that emanated from it. It was also an action – above all other challenges that Jesus made to the religious and political authorities – that led to his arrest, trials and execution.

So where can we find God? McVerry urges us to look in a different direction and for a different God:

Jesus announced a God who was not separated from God's people. Far from it. God was to be found there in the sick, the poor, the blind, the lame, the man robbed and beaten. God *identified* with the people. For Jesus, holiness consists not in separation from sinners but in proximity to sinners.[51]

Have we, the Christian community of solidarity with each other, chosen to locate God back into our churches, the new Temple, the new Holy of Holies, and once again surrounded God with priests? Has sacred space once again been safely separated from those who make us uncomfortable: the poor, the unwanted, the despised? Once again, do we restrict access to God through priests and place the poor and marginalised in the margins? Have we removed God from the streets, the market place, from people's homes and from their dinner tables and locked God in our tabernacles? And what would the young rabbi from Nazareth think if he returned to see how we have made God 'safe' by removing Him from life, by separating Him from people, especially from the lowly and the poor? What would Jesus make of our fascination with rules and regulations, with our judging those who are 'outside the Law'? Would he share our admiration for ornate church buildings? What would he make of the Vatican? Are we – good solid practising Christians – completely immune from Jesus' famous judgement on Temple worship or have we too, by neglecting and excluding the poor, by 'privatising' God and by giving preference to ritual, rule and institution over Spirit and Truth, not also created our own form of Temple worship?

Chapter 13

A Mother's Plea: 'Leave my Child Alone!'

I NEVER SAW an African child as the latest fashion accessory until I went to Africa and met people at both ends of the charity/justice volunteering dichotomy. The Project Zambia immersion groups often tend to fly from Belfast on a Friday, arriving (via Heathrow) in Lusaka around dawn on the following Saturday. Some of the lucky volunteers are able to put their heads down for a few hours in the hostel and catch up with a bit of missed sleep. Those who were silly enough to volunteer as 'leadership team' spend these precious hours getting money changed, buying water and other essential goods and making contact with our host communities to ensure that the programme runs as planned. The afternoon is spent visiting the immersion sites and getting people's heads around the fact that they are in a Third World country and that they are now dislocated from everything their Western lifestyle presumed. On Sunday we rise at an early hour to be in time for the morning mass in the St Lawrence Community Centre in Misisi. After the most incredible liturgical celebration and connection with our African brothers and sisters, we are taken for a journey through the Misisi slum to acquaint the new volunteers with life in the margins in Africa. We follow Peter Tembo through the narrow lanes of Misisi – passing among the hovels in which so many people in this part of the world are condemned to live and die in, carefully avoid falling into the open sewers and stepping over the excrement and dead rats that lie all around – and smile at and laugh with the children who run after the line of *bazungu* who have entered their world. And then, on one of these visits, I took the hand of a child.

The mother in Misisi whose child's hand I was holding ran out from her hut in a rage. I was at the front of the *bazungu* line so all she could see was her daughter holding a tall *muzungu's* hand in the middle of her world. She firmly removed my hand from her daughter's and launched into a burst of Nyanja that I can only presume was not entirely complimentary. Then Peter Tembo arrived on the scene and things became much clearer to all of us. 'Do not steal our children!' she had been shouting at us before she became aware that this was not our intention. At first I was taken aback and ashamed that this is what her initial understanding of our presence in Misisi had been. The poor mother believed that I was like many of the *bazungu* who visit such communities with the intention of adopting a child. Some do it out of a naïve sense of misguided compassion. They believe that by taking one child out of poverty they are in some way making a positive contribution to the plight of the victims of poverty. It is, however, precisely the opposite. This form of meddling in the lives of those in the margins does nothing other than portray those who live in dire poverty as helpless and passive objects of pity, whose escape from a miserable life of squalor and despair lies in the hands and power of affluent benefactors who may 'rescue' one of these 'unfortunates' from their misery and bring them to the salvation of the affluent West. It reinforces the notion that the situation of those in poverty-stricken countries throughout the world is hopeless to the point that meaningful change in their societies is impossible. It neither addresses the causes of the humanitarian crisis nor contemplates its solution. According to the United Nations Children's Fund (UNICEF), there are one hundred and forty-three million orphans in sub-Saharan Africa, Asia, Latin America and the Caribbean.[52] This equates to one in thirteen children in the Developing World – and this number is rising fast. According to the UN, between 1990 and 2010 the number of children orphaned by AIDS in sub-Saharan Africa will have risen from less than one million to more than fifteen million, which amounts to one in five children in some southern African states. This will not be mollified or solved by people from the affluent West, many no doubt sincere in their desire to do something good, going to poverty-stricken regions of the world and 'selecting' one child for salvation – a 'winner' in a lottery created by the 'generosity' of the sponsor. Angela Miyanda points out that the HIV/AIDS pandemic and other aspects of poverty have destroyed countless families in Africa. This 'solution' – of breaking up yet another family (extended or otherwise) by adopting a child, removing it from its home and community and whisking it off to a new life in the West – may not be as simple and beneficial as it may appear. It leads to Africa being treated like a helpless orphan child who requires adoption by the affluent West – the very society that created and maintains the inhuman conditions endured by those in the margins. Ultimately, it leads to an acceptance of the unacceptable. An orphan here and there, lucky enough to be plucked from poverty, suffices to salve the conscience of the affluent world.

The latest fashion accessory: a cute African child

There is an even darker side to extraterritorial adoption than the one associated with the misguided and misplaced sense of pity outlined above: the idea of the Third World orphan child as a fashion accessory. The trend of celebrities adopting children from the poorest regions in the world was started by Angelina Jolie, the actress and UN Good Will Ambassador, who adopted a Cambodian orphan in 2001 and an Ethiopian child (who was allegedly not an orphan) in 2005. However, it was the hugely publicised adoption by the pop singer, Madonna, of a one-year-old baby from an orphanage in Malawi in 2006 that raised serious questions and concerns of such practices in the minds of many. No doubt the adopted child, David, will live in comfort and have a materially privileged life. Supporters of the pop singer will, no doubt, point out that, for this child at least, life will be better. That is no excuse. Despite the headlines, this boy was not an orphan; his mother had died a month after birth due to post-natal problems associated with poverty. The baby was living in an orphanage simply because his father could not afford to feed him. David has a real family in Malawi. His father, thiry-one-year-old Yohane Banda, is a Christian peasant farmer who carves wooden axe handles to make a living. Staff at the orphanage said he regularly cycled twenty-five kilometres through the dust to see his son. The adoption process itself makes uncomfortable reading. Apparently the pop singer asked the orphanage to email pictures of twelve children and, from the list, she chose David. A couple of days later she flew to Malawi, inspected the child, declared him 'beautiful' and then went to court to make the adoption official. Mr Banda went to court wearing stained trousers and a check shirt. Madonna wore a simple black dress and knee-high black boots. After the court gave Madonna temporary custody, she flew out of Malawi. A day later, she had her employees deliver the toddler to her London home. In total, the whirlwind spending spree cost Madonna around $6 million, for which she not only picked up an African child but the whole orphanage, which she'd agreed to sponsor. Her husband, the film producer Guy Ritchie, got to make a documentary about poverty in Malawi. Winners all round? Somehow, I think not.

One could make the point that $6 million would have lifted Mr Banda's entire village out of poverty. Some may suggest that Madonna's approach is selfish, vulgar and crass (especially due to the fact that the boy's family was assured that Madonna was a 'good Christian woman'). Yet, how was whisking this young African child out of his village in front of the world media addressing the orphan problem in Africa? The symbolism of the act – a rich, white woman removing a child from its home and culture – seems to me to smack of a new kind of slavery. For centuries, commencing in the mid-fifteenth century when Portuguese interests in Africa moved away from the fabled deposits of gold to a much more readily available commodity – people – Africa's 'human resources' were ruthlessly mined according to the economic priorities of the expanding European empires, peaking in the eighteenth century when more than six million Africans were taken as slaves, with Britain the worst transgressor being responsible for transporting two and a half million slaves.[53] Once this ended, its physical resources were targeted. And now, its children are the targets.

'We've just found a cute black child that might suit Mildred and John'

It's not just the rich and famous who engage in this crass and highly questionable 'select a lucky orphan' scenario. They are simply following a trend that has been going on for a number of years – although in the case of the celebrity adoptive parents, it is carried out in full media glare. Children have been adopted by people from the affluent West in considerable numbers from countries such as Romania, Russia, India, Nepal, Pakistan, Sri Lanka and Bangladesh, as well as a host of countries in Latin America and Africa. Often this is a natural reaction by people, moved by feeling considerable sorrow for children in such circumstances and wanting to give them a better life. For example, when the harrowing images of neglected and emaciated boys and girls, their heads shaved to prevent the spread of lice, were broadcasted from Romanian orphanages in 1989, it prompted an influx of international aid and requests for adoption to the West. But the images also helped to encourage a not so philanthropic if, perhaps misguided, activity, as these children began to be exported for sale to couples abroad who wanted to adopt. As this international trade in children grew, so too did the power of the criminal gangs at its centre.

Impoverished families were coerced and deceived into giving up their children, who were then effectively sold on to Western couples under the guise of international adoption. The fate of many children who undergo this process is even worse as some children, exported abroad, often against their will, are subjected to paedophilia, child prostitution or domestic servitude.[54] This international trading of children has grown enormously over the past two decades – as has the power and influence of the criminal gangs that organise it. These young vulnerable people are then sold off under the guise of international adoption, in the hope of a better life. Human trafficking has become a big business.[55] However, it is not just the criminal gangs who are involved in removing children from their families and communities and exporting them to the West. Transnational adoption is now a huge industry involving lawyers, government officials, local representatives and many other key players. Sometimes, while working in the undeveloped world, one does come across some people and organisations who remind you that the poor mother in Misisi who shouted 'do not steal our children' was not imagining things.[56]

I had just arrived in a backpacker hostel outside of Lusaka and I noticed that there was a large group of people from the USA there. It didn't take me too long to figure out that I had bumped into a volunteer group (uniform tee shirts and logos told me that) who were in Africa to 'do something'. The briefest conversation confirmed to me that they were an evangelical fundamentalist group. Their organisation was going to spend nine months in total in Zambia with groups of volunteers being replaced every four weeks. They informed me that they had a building project 'somewhere just outside Lusaka'. There was something about this group that just didn't seem right. Most volunteering groups tend to have a youngish profile. Such is the nature of volunteering that it often attracts younger adults like gap-year students, those who have just left university and other young people who have not quite yet entered the whole life-career structure. Of course, others from every age group and life stage are also to be found working in projects in the Developing World. Some, having completed a considerable number of years working in the West, decide that it is time to try to make a difference to people who live in poverty or who are otherwise disadvantaged. Others are attracted by the challenge of going somewhere completely different and doing something completely different. The people who belonged to this organisation – and I actually met three different cohorts of this group at different times in Zambia – were strange indeed. First of all, they were predominantly (but not exclusively) middle-aged females and decidedly materially well-off. They all seemed to be so precisely the same in outlook, attitude and behaviour that you would have thought they had been cloned in some military establishment and been programmed to take part in some sociological experiment. While it may seem apparent that organisations of a certain ethos will tend to attract people of a similar outlook and world vision, these people were of an exceptionally uniform and similar nature. They didn't seem too interested in the type of work Project Zambia was involved in ... except when we mentioned orphanages.

For people who suddenly became quite interested about our work in Africa, especially when we mentioned the word 'orphans' or 'orphanage', they proved to be quite reticent in providing information about where they were based and what they actually did during the day in Africa. A bus came for them around 7.30 a.m. and took them away 'somewhere' and returned them at 4.30 in the afternoon. What had occurred or been achieved during those hours of daylight was not forthcoming, despite having had numerous conversations with the volunteers: 'I don't really know where we go during the day. I just get on the bus and fall asleep'. How far away is their base? Again I get a shrug of the shoulders and a smile: 'I don't bother much with time or that stuff'. I observe the rather fancy US timepiece on a wrist: 'Well, which direction is it? Up the Great North Road? The Great East Road, perhaps? Towards Kafue? Manda Hill direction?' I get a blank look and a mumbled comment that my friend doesn't pay too much attention to roads, districts or village names, roundabouts or any identifiable building, distinguishing feature or any other point of reference. At least all of my new friends were direct and uniform in telling me what they did during the day: 'We're building houses for poor people somewhere up there', was the standard (almost rehearsed) reply. The problem I had with that answer is that, while trying not to disbelieve the speaker, normally when one is engaged with construction in Africa one comes back from a day's work pretty fatigued and very much covered in red dust and cement. The welcomed shower after a day spent in the slums or villages in Africa reveals just how much of the sand, soil and orchid dust you carry back with you. The water runs red as you separate the day's labour from your body. However, when these guys came back each day there was scarce evidence that they had spent much time anywhere near physical work or any other such activity. I had never discovered what they actually did, as each time, just when I thought one of them, usually one of the younger ones, was about to reveal something, one of the leaders would apologise for the interruption, and always with the sincerest smile on his/her face: 'But we have a team meeting starting just now and don't worry because it'll be over soon and you guys will get back to finish your conversation in no time'. Well, 'no time' never came and I never got to finish those conversations or find out what these guys did ... until I met Pete.

Pete the attorney

Pete stood out from the rest of this group. He was middle-aged, male and seemed to be actively looking out for people to engage with. He also, quite uniquely being with a born-again Christian group, would appear in the small bar area in the hostel with a bottle of beer in his hand. The rest of his party were at a group meeting and some of the Project Zambia people were having a bit of a sing-song in the communal area, while others were playing cards, journaling and talking about the day's experiences. He introduced himself and seemed friendly enough and glad of some company. I also suspect that he had had a couple of beers already as, unlike the others we had met, Pete was pretty forthcoming with information about himself and the group he was with and what they were about. He wasn't actually a member of the group, he informed us. His bottle of beer appeared to suggest that anyway. He was over with his wife (who was a fully fledged member of the church group) and was just happy to share a few stories over a drink with his new Irish buddies. Pete informed us that he was an attorney back in the US, specialising in adoption laws. He was over in Zambia 'tidying up some legal stuff on behalf of my wife and her guys. You have to make sure all the papers are in order for the immigration people'. One of our people mentioned that we were working in some of the orphanages too. His interest was immediate but faded when he discovered that our main contacts in Zambia were the Christian Brothers, the White Fathers and the Sisters of the Sacred Heart. 'Those orphanages run by the priests and nuns are a problem', sighed Pete. 'I mean, when we try to visit one of those places and ask about adopting some of the children, we don't get past first base.' And it wasn't just the Catholic religious orders who pointed these people to the door. Mrs Miyanda, herself a member of a Pentecostal Church, viewed such practices with equal hostility and suspicion. For people such as Angela, adoption, unless it is to access medical care that is unavailable in Zambia or if it is unsafe for an orphan to remain in the country, is anathema to her and most certainly not a means of overcoming poverty and the growing orphan crisis in Africa. At best, it is well intentioned but misguided love. More often, however, it is another injustice visited on the marginalised and oppressed. At worst, it is affluent Westerners playing the 'orphan lottery'. 'Which orphan will I pick? Which cute one will I save? The young girl with the big appealing eyes, the wee boy with the mischievous and cheeky look or the kid over there who looks sad and lost? Eeny, meeny, miny, mo ...'[57]

I tried to suggest to Pete that people like those whom he was with, who go around the slums, shanty towns and impoverished villages in the Third World selecting orphans for adoption, were actually playing God – and a very nasty God at that. They were deciding which child would become one of the elect and, therefore, be 'saved' from a miserable and damned life of poverty and suffering, which a multitude of children would not. They were also defining salvation. To be saved was to become Westernised: to be elevated to the affluent West and adopt the Western dream, the Western lifestyle and Western values. Yet, it is precisely this dream, this lifestyle and these values that have created and condemned Africa and the rest of the Third World to the crushing poverty from which they seek to escape.

Pete wasn't catching my drift at all. He seemed pretty focused on his designated purpose and role. He was the attorney brought there to sort out the legal bits and pieces 'in order to ensure that the transfer of the kids goes as planned'. At this stage in the conversation, I hoped that Pete would stop and realise the fact that the USA does indeed include in its population a rather large number of Afro-Americans, who are the direct descendants of people from Africa who, like the adopted orphans, were not in control of their own destiny. Their ancestors did not just jump onto a boat in west Africa and sail to America in order to find a 'better life'. Rather, they were captured, brutalised, tortured, raped, humiliated, transported and sold. They were enslaved and sold as just that: slaves. Pete had no interest at all in the Afro-American diaspora, nor in single mothers or their children, the elderly, the abandoned, junkies, tramps, alcoholics, ex/current prisoners, or any other person or sector that does not hit the middle-class radar of social acceptability and 'chicness'. In the most bizarre and weird reversal of the traditional way in which many in the affluent white upper/middle classes view and respond to marginalised sectors of society in the United States (and many other places in the world), here was Pete – and his group – searching Africa for 'cute' orphans to adopt. Certainly, Pete didn't seem to fit into our mindset. As the evening wore on, Pete became more open about the nature and purpose of the group he had accompanied and his role within it. Some were over to adopt children for themselves; others were there to identify potential children for members of their church/social network in the USA. Overall, their organisation was seeking to set up a network, structure and contact that would facilitate such practices in the future. It was my eldest daughter, Caoimhe, who recalled hearing someone of this group on the phone to their people back in the USA enthusiastically passing on the news that they had identified 'a cute little black child that might suit Mildred and John'. They then went on to reassure them that the photos of the child would be emailed over the very next day so Mildred and John could have a look at the images before my new friend Pete would swing into action.

Becoming Fully Immersed

Experiences in Mapepe

Chapter 14

Off the Beaten Track to Mapepe

A new challenge

IT WAS FR OSWALD, the parish priest of Kabwata and Misisi,
who introduced me to this place. He had come across the
name 'Mapepe' while carrying out his function as chaplain
in the main prison in Lusaka. Mapepe can be accurately
described as a rural slum. Situated twenty-five kilometres
south of Lusaka and just off the main road to Livingstone,
Mapepe is much like any other community in sub-Saharan
Africa that progress and development has bypassed. For the
people of Mapepe, the road from Lusaka to Livingstone
(part of the Cape to Cairo network that goes the whole
length of Africa) does not exist, as it doesn't take them
anywhere. Of course, it goes past them; it just doesn't bring
them anywhere. Hence we have lorries, coaches, minibuses
and all other forms of vehicles going from/to every country
in Africa passing communities that haven't changed in
hundreds of years. Their struggle for survival continues:
bypassed, hidden and ignored.

'God has given us another challenge, Aidan.' Every time
Fr Oswald, the young missionary from Tanzania, says or
writes this to me I say to myself, 'Sweet Lord, what now?'

and then I say (or write), 'Of course, Father. Let us trust in the Holy Spirit. It doesn't set us tasks we cannot meet, does it, Father?' It was Fr Oswald who taught me that, so he's hardly going to go against his own advice and, lest I weaken in my trust of such leaps of faith, Fr Oswald will always direct me to *Lumen Gentium* or the relevant sections of the *Catechism of the Catholic Church* to assure me that we are not acting alone but under the guidance of the Holy Spirit. There is something theologically simplistic yet simultaneously profound and challenging to the advice from Fr Oswald. At one level, it almost reveals a child-like innocence and trust in providence and in the continual presence and guidance of the Holy Spirit. Yet, on the other hand, this is precisely what we proclaim when we invoke the Holy Spirit through praying:

> Come Holy Spirit, and fill the hearts of your faithful, and kindle in them the fire of Your Divine Love. Send forth Your Spirit and they shall be created, and You shall renew the face of the earth.

All Fr Oswald challenges us to do is take what we say we proclaim or profess to believe seriously. In other words, if we do really believe in the Holy Spirit and that it guides the Church and us in the building of the kingdom, perhaps we should start to listen a bit more to where the Spirit is calling us.

Fr Oswald explained to me that while visiting the prisoners in Lusaka Central Prison he was struck by the horrendous conditions these unfortunate souls are forced to endure. Like most prisons in Africa, those in Zambia are chronically overcrowded and lack access to medical care, which should be provided by law. The failure to remove or quarantine sick prisoners results in the spreading of airborne illnesses, such as tuberculosis. They are also malnourished, due largely to the fact that prisoners receive only one serving of corn meal and beans per day, called a 'combined meal' because it represents breakfast, lunch and dinner. Violence is a constant threat, as is the occurrence of rape, adding to an already high HIV/AIDS rate. In a human rights report on Zambia compiled in 2007 by the US Bureau of Democracy, Human Rights and Labour, the following was concluded:

> Prison conditions were poor and life threatening. An inefficient judiciary delayed court proceedings and exacerbated overcrowding. The country's prisons, which were built to hold 5,500 inmates, held nearly 14,600 prisoners. Lusaka Central Prison, which was designed to accommodate 200 prisoners, held more than 1,200 inmates, forcing some inmates to sleep sitting upright. Poor sanitation, inadequate medical facilities, meagre food supplies, and lack of potable water resulted in serious outbreaks of dysentery, cholera, and tuberculosis, which were compounded by overcrowding.[58]

It is little wonder that those who are in such prisons look forward to the day when they are able to leave such conditions and return to their families.

'But not Mapepe, Aidan', Fr Oswald told me. 'The inmates from Mapepe', he continued, 'tell me that they do not want to go back. There is no life there. At least in prison they get something to eat. They prefer to stay!' Fr Oswald could not believe what he was being told by the prisoners, so he went to Mapepe to see for himself. He asked me to go with him and we were accompanied by four young Zambian catechists, just out of university. Their names are Cecilia, Derek, Osten and Yvonne and they had decided to devote the next couple of years to working with and for the marginalised in keeping with the challenge issued by Jesus to all of us in the Gospel of Matthew:

> I was hungry and you fed me, thirsty and you gave me a drink; I was a stranger and you received me in your homes, naked and you clothed me; I was sick and you took care of me, in prison and you visited me.
>
> (Matthew 25:35-36)

In Mapepe they found a challenge worthy of any follower of the Gospel.

The unmistakable presence of poverty

Conditions in Mapepe are dire indeed. The population of some two thousand people is crammed into a tiny area of land, with no access to medical or meaningful educational facilities, appalling sanitation and a single hand pump for drinking water for the whole population. The houses, such as they are, are made of mud bricks of extremely poor quality or asbestos pipes from the old sewage system. All agriculture is of a meagre sustenance nature – and hopelessly inadequate even at that – and there are no income generating projects whatsoever. In short, this is an

163

abandoned people: the wretched of the earth. Nothing, I suspect, save a famine or war, could make their daily lives worse.

At the same time, for all its dire poverty, there is something dangerously illusory about an impoverished rural community that one doesn't encounter in an urban slum. Slums in the cities or shanty towns appear exactly as they are: inhuman, filthy, ugly and poverty-stricken hell holes, where the abandoned of the world are crammed into and forgotten about. The 2009 film *Slumdog Millionaire* portrays the appalling squalor of the slums of Mumbai perfectly and clearly illustrates the universal experience of living in such conditions. While watching the film in the cinema, I was transported back to Misisi, Kabwata, Kamwala, Kibera, Embulbul or any of the other slums I have stepped into in Africa. Strangely, it was not the images of the slums in *Slumdog Millionaire* that reawakened my awareness; it was the sense of smell. You do not see a slum in a city – you *smell* it.

In the West, we have a strong visually focused sense of apprehending and accessing reality. We look and see, and whatever we see – especially in our twenty-four-hour satellite dominated media world – is real and true. We are sold or, in truth, we buy into a version of the world that is presented to us by the mass media of advertising, satellite news, popular press and reality television. In our fragmented, noisy and impatient world we often do not listen to each other. We sometimes catch snatches of conversation, but we often do not pay attention long enough to develop a narrative. We seem to be always moving on to the next snatch of conversation or topic. Even our understanding of the lives of those in the margins is given to us as images, either as stark pictures of victims of poverty or through documentaries or film clips of a far away and different world. The images we see and the picture we develop in our minds of living in poverty is only partial. We cannot really enter the world of the margins through images. Indeed, the more images we see the less able we become to access this world because we become less shocked by and more desensitised to the living conditions the victims of poverty are forced to live in. The overwhelming stench of a slum, on the other hand, allows us to experience the reality of such conditions to an altogether higher degree, so much so that you can almost *feel* poverty. The unforgettable pungent stench of waste welcomes visitors at the entrance to any urban slum or village in the undeveloped world. Sewage, human, animal and household waste all end up in the alleys, waterways and oozing sewers throughout the slums, which leads to illnesses of all kinds for the residents. Frequent floods due to inadequate public sewage works exacerbate the problems for the slum dwellers as well. The stench not only gets into your nostrils, it also seems to attach itself to your hair, your skin and your clothes. Even taking a shower after having spent time somewhere like Kibera or Misisi does not remove the odour of poverty. It clings to you like a reminder of your visit there and doesn't go away easily.

Perhaps we in the Developed World should not be so surprised at this. Poverty – be it the desperate absolute poverty in the slums and villages of the undeveloped world or the 'relative' poverty found in the soulless housing estates and isolated rural areas in the apparently well-off affluent world – is a singular concept and common experience. Poverty involves not just economic and material factors and indicators, it also involves deeply social, personal and spiritual aspects of life. Poverty is about hopelessness. It is about not seeing a way forward – a future. Poverty is about giving up, about accepting the grinding reality of the conditions that one lives in and not fighting back. Poverty, locally and globally, is not difficult to recognise. It presents itself as that sense of powerlessness that reduces the victim to a state of passivity and quiet despair. The poverty of those in the margins can indeed be felt.

Mapepe: dire poverty in a pretty setting

Rural poverty, on the other hand, can often be disguised by the beauty of the setting in which it exists. The village of Mapepe, for example, is a case in point. Situated in a river valley and surrounded by rolling hills with lush forestation in abundance, it seems almost idyllic. The mud dwelling places, with their thatched roofs and grass fences, seem to evoke another era and have a timeless quality about them. Certainly, they present a marked contrast to the soulless and crumbling block hovels with their sheets of plastic and corrugated tin or asbestos roofs of Misisi. Even the people of Mapepe, especially the children, appear to have avoided the harshness and violence of urban slum living. Indeed, looking at the women singing as they wait their turn at the water pump, watching the barefoot children at play and listening to the men engaged in deep conversation under the shade of a tree or in a rondavel, one can very easily conjure up images of the eighteenth-century Swiss philosopher Jean-Jacques Rousseau's idealisation of what he considered to be the original state of nature and the hypothetical state of humankind in it.[59] However, one would be entirely wrong. Images, perceptions and appearances can, indeed, be misleading. Rural poverty can be every bit as grinding, overwhelming and crushing as its urban counterpart. Indeed, such is the poverty and hopelessness of rural village life that, for many, life in an urban slum, with all its hazards, dangers and drawbacks, is a better option. Life in a village like Mapepe is indeed tough. A key socio-economic indicator of development is infant and child mortality rates. In Zambia, the main causes for high infant and child mortality are diarrhoea, malnutrition, malaria, HIV and acute respiratory infections. These are as common in rural as in urban settings. Indeed, rural areas often find themselves disadvantaged in relation to food security, health provision, education and economic growth than their urban counterparts. If the rains fail and you live in a rural community, prepare for drought and famine. If your child becomes ill and you live in a village, be prepared to carry your child to the nearest medical centre (presuming you have the money to pay for medicine and doctor's fees). Otherwise, place your faith in a witch doctor. If you want your child to gain an education, expect that child to have to walk a considerable number of miles each day to go to the nearest school. As for any meaningful income generation projects that might break the chains of poverty – forget it.

The industrialised world, with its economic dominance, mass production facilities, scale of economies and ability to develop and exploit markets throughout the world, ensures that the chronically underdeveloped infrastructures and fragile economies of countries such as those in sub-Saharan

Africa have no chance of 'playing on a level playing field'. The outcome is as predetermined as a match between Manchester United and Aidan Donaldson's Select. And if by some miracle or outrageous fluke Aidan Donaldson's Select are managing to beat their more famous and richer opponents, then the referee will intervene to ensure that the natural order is restored. Again, if by some equally remarkable circumstance the referee fails to act in the interests of the powerful, the rules will be changed to facilitate the pre-ordained result.

In her 2007 work, *The Shock Doctrine: the Rise of Disaster Capitalism*, a chilling, revelatory and scathing attack on corporate acquisitiveness that is ravaging the planet, the Canadian author and political activist, Naomi Klein, argues that corporate capitalism employs every necessary weapon in its desire to globalise and remake the world in its own image and likeness. According to Klein:

> [Corporatism's] main characteristics [include] huge transfers of public wealth to private hands, often accompanied by exploding debt, an ever-widening chasm between the dazzling rich and the disposable poor and an aggressive nationalism that justifies bottomless spending on security. For those inside the bubble of extreme wealth created by such an arrangement, there can be no more profitable way to organise a society. But because of the obvious drawbacks for the vast majority of the population left outside the bubble, other features of the corporatist state tend to include aggressive surveillance (with government and large corporations trading favours

and contracts), mass incarceration, shrinking civil liberties and, often, though not always, torture.[60]

Klein further points out that this system does not shrink from employing military force if necessary and 'has harnessed the full force of the US military machine in the service of a corporate agenda'.[61] As evidence of 'the rise of disaster capitalism', Klein cites no-bid service contracts announced for ExxonMobil, Chevron, Shell, BP and Total in 2008, through which the vast oil reserves of Iraq will fall under foreign ownership; the outsourcing of the 'War on Terror' to private 'military companies' such as Blackwater (now called Xe) and oil corporations such as Halliburton; the auctioning off of the beaches of Southeast Asia to the tourist industry after the tsunami of December 2004; and the sale of the New Orleans school system to private education companies and corporations after Hurricane Katrina.[62] Faced with such daunting and crushing economic and political forces, it is little wonder that the impoverished countries of the undeveloped world are unable to compete in any meaningful way with the globalised economies of the affluent 'bubble' and continue to fall behind the West both in real and relative terms.

Mapepe, the Gospel and liberation

So, what chance, therefore, has a community in the margins of the already marginalised, such as Mapepe, got of transforming itself? Actually, quite a lot. Despite all of the all too obvious disadvantages, communities such as Mapepe – or any other slum such as Misisi for that matter – contain the seeds of their own salvation from poverty. While it is clear that it is multinational globalised capitalism that has created and maintains the inhuman conditions that much of the world's population is forced to exist in, the struggle of these communities is more basic and pressing than simply patiently awaiting the collapse of that economic system. The forgotten people of the margins desperately seek a future for their children, a dignified stage of old age for their elderly, comfort for their sick and, lastly, a better life for themselves. The key to the transformation of oppressed people's lives is education. No people should understand this better than the Irish. After all, was it not education that lifted the Irish from their state of dire poverty, desperation, oppression and servitude in the post-famine period, to become the confident and independent nation that has contributed much to the modern world? Not least of the gifts that Ireland has given to the world have been the large number of missionaries – ordained, religious and lay – who have made a real difference to those whose situation reminds us all of our own relatively recent history. The importance of education in the struggle against poverty is most certainly not lost on those who live in the margins. They live their problems and they know the solution.

Those in the margins full well understand the immediate challenges that face the people: HIV/AIDS and other illnesses, the orphan crisis, lack of food and medical facilities, sanitation and access to adequate water supplies. Yet, in every single village or urban slum I have visited and sat down with the community leaders, the community always return to one issue: 'Can we build a school? Without this our children do not have a future'. And they are absolutely correct. Mapepe is no different. Everything in terms of community development is directed towards prioritising education and making it sustainable. This is precisely where organisations such as Project Zambia (and, of course, much larger NGOs, governmental agencies and other partners) must step up to the mark and realise their role is in helping to bring this about. Host communities need two things from justice volunteers in order for them to change their world. The first is financial support that will empower them to start to realise their plans and dreams. In many ways funding is a catalyst without which their hopes would remain unfulfilled. As it is absolutely impossible for an impoverished community to raise its own initial funds for any project, be it educational, income generating or basic health provision, it is a task that we, who have access to such funding, have to take up. And a relatively small amount of money can go a long way in the undeveloped world if it is channelled properly. The second is that the host communities do not want to be passive recipients of the generosity of anonymous donors or benefactors. They wish to work in partnership with their supporters and, in so doing, together we affirm one another in solidarity, mutual recognition and love. This latter activity is, if anything, even more important than fundraising because it is through this process of mutual affirmation that a radical empowerment of the community comes about. The hitherto forgotten people at the margins come to see themselves as no longer abandoned and forgotten. Through immersion they (and we) have encountered that human defining and social transforming concept: hope.

'So what exactly have these *bazungu* given you guys?'

Tom Kearney is on the Christian Brothers' African Province Leadership Team. An Australian who has spent quite a number of years in Africa, he is nobody's fool. I met Tom for the first time when I was in Kenya and we seemed to get on pretty well. Social justice and immersion were two themes that seemed to intertwine and mean the same for both of us. So when I found out that he had been moved to Lusaka in June to organise the formation centre for young novices, I became very interested indeed. I figured out that since the Christian Brothers didn't have mission stations in Lusaka itself, Tom might be interested in looking at some of the projects that Project Zambia was involved with. I'd be in Lusaka in July so I could see how we might develop this further.

Tom picked me up at the side of the Great East Road near the centre of Lusaka. 'Good', I thought to myself, 'he's brought the Christian Brothers' minibus with high clearance. We'll need it. We're going to Mapepe.' Driving down the dirt road into Mapepe in a car during July just about might be okay, provided that you avoid the potholes and rocks that protrude after the rainy season. Trying to drive up and out of Mapepe might be an altogether different experience and good luck to the first guy to try it. Anyway, with Tom and his minibus, any potential fear I might have had about trying to get a vehicle out of Mapepe and back on the road to Lusaka was put firmly out of my mind. We stepped out of the minibus outside the old school. All around was a frenzy of activity. It seemed that all the people of Mapepe had joined forces with the immersion volunteers because the foundations for the new school were being dug, the piggery was pretty close to roof level and an extension to the agricultural programme was being created. 'Goodness me,' said Tom, 'there's something going on here and I'm going to find out what it is.' He then set about going round all of the projects and speaking with anyone who would stop work long enough to engage in conversation. He finally came to Mr Mulenga, Chairperson of the Mapepe Community Development Committee. 'Okay, Mr Mulenga, I see that your people are really making great progress here. What would you say is the most important thing that these *bazungu* have contributed to your community?' Mr Mulenga looked around at the various projects under development. I wondered what he might identify as Project Zambia's most significant contribution to his village. Would it be money without which none of the building materials could have been bought? Perhaps Mr Mulenga might pick out one project like the water pump, the new school, the chicken run or some other venture that has made a real difference to the people of Mapepe. Mr Mulenga turned to Tom and smiled. 'Yes,' he said, 'our Irish brothers and sisters have made a great difference to my people. They have brought with them the gift of hope.' He was right and wise. Without hope nothing can grow.

Hope and the kingdom

It is this transforming and liberating concept of hope that lies at the heart of every movement that has striven for change and justice throughout history. The startling demand delivered by Aaron, the elder brother of Moses, to Pharaoh in Exodus (5:1) – 'Let my people go' – is not simply a demand that can be limited to one event in history. It is, in fact, a universal demand that must be applied to every situation in human history when people's humanity is denied. It was that single thought, that stirring of the spirit, that lead people to seek to transcend their conditions. The same one that unites people such as Sparticus, who led the great revolt against slavery in ancient Rome, Ghandi, who freed India from the yoke of imperialism, Martin Luther King, so important in the struggle for civil rights in the United States, and Nelson Mandela and Steve Biko, who led the black consciousness movement in South Africa against the indignity and cruelty of the human-denying apartheid regime. And it is hope – the anticipation, imagining and dreaming of a new and better future – that excites and stirs the human spirit. Without hope there is no transformation, or, as the scripture writer tells us, 'Where there is no vision the people perish' (Proverbs 29:18).

This striving for transformation sparked by hope is the central teaching of Christianity, from the moment when John the Baptist urged the people to 'Repent, for the kingdom of God is at hand' (Mark 1:15). This becomes even clearer and more dramatic when Jesus announces his ministry with such urgency when asked to read from the scriptures in the synagogue in Nazareth (Luke 4:14-21). Whether Jesus deliberately selected the famous prophetic passage from Isaiah 61 or whether it was simply a preselected passage following a strict cycle of readings is unknown and irrelevant. How Jesus read and commented on the passage, however, is of immense importance. The piece of Old Testament scripture is rich and pregnant with images of the coming of the kingdom. Let us consider again Luke's account of the event:

Jesus returned to Galilee in the power of the Spirit, and news about him spread through the whole countryside. He taught in their synagogues, and everyone praised him. He went to Nazareth, where he had been brought up, and on the Sabbath day he went into the synagogue, as was his custom. The scroll of the prophet Isaiah was handed to him. Unrolling it, he found the place where it is written:
'The Spirit of the Lord is on me, because he has anointed me to preach good news to the poor. He has sent me to proclaim freedom for the prisoners and recovery of sight for the blind, to release the oppressed, to proclaim the year of the Lord's favour.'

(Luke 4:16-19)

At this stage, Jesus has not done anything out of the ordinary or controversial. The audience, no doubt, would have pondered deeply, nodded assent seriously and, perhaps, waited for the young rabbi to complete the reading. After all, Jesus had actually finished reading on a comma. What Jesus did and said, however, certainly 'disturbed the peace' of many devout listeners and gives us today many things to consider:

Then he rolled up the scroll, gave it back to the attendant and sat down. The eyes of everyone in the synagogue were fastened on him, and he began by saying to them, 'Today this scripture is fulfilled in your hearing.'

(Luke 4:20)

The fact that Jesus didn't finish the reading – stopping mid-sentence – is of crucial importance. The actual reading from Isaiah continues with the promise of 'a day of revenge for the Lord' and other suggestions that the kingdom would (a) be in the future and (b) be brought about by God. Jesus, however, said no such thing. The kingdom was being created as he spoke. Indeed, all throughout his revelation, Jesus proclaimed the kingdom with an urgency that does not allow for waiting for the kingdom to arrive at some day of God's choosing: 'The time is now'; 'The Kingdom is near'; 'Repent and believe in the Good News'. Jesus' answer at his trial before the Sanhedrin to the question posed by the High Priest, Caiaphas, 'Are you the Christ, Son of the Blessed One?' (Mark 14:61), is a most extraordinary and revolutionary statement indeed. According to the Gospel of Mark, Jesus answered as follows:

> I am. And you will see the Son of Man sitting at the right hand of the Power and coming with the clouds of heaven.
>
> (Mark 14:62)

Caiaphas was left with no choice, not that he wanted one. This man had to be destroyed. After all, in putting himself forward as the Christ, the Messiah, in, for example, his entry into Jerusalem and in identifying himself as the Son of Man of the prophecy from the Book of Daniel which proclaimed a final judgement, Jesus was announcing the Kingdom of God and calling an end to the corrupt Temple worship and the exclusion of the poor and the marginalised from this kingdom. This latter demand – one that infuses and drives Jesus' mission – was impossible for the Jewish (and Roman) authorities to tolerate. According to Peter McVerry:

If the People of God failed to exclude these sinners, the People of God would become, like them, impure. Then the wrath of God would be visited on the whole People of God, and the unique relationship that the Covenant created between the Chosen People and God would be at risk, and therefore Israel's very existence as a nation, which was founded on that Covenant, would be in jeopardy.[63]

In many ways, Jesus had immersed himself with the poor and outsiders. He ate with them (Mark 2:16-17). He sought out their company, including tax collectors like Zacchaeus, women 'who had been cured of evil spirits and infirmities' (Luke 8:2), non-Jews and even the hated oppressors, the Romans. He forgave sin and cured the sick as in the story of the paralytic (Mark 2:1-12) and associated with the most marginalised of all at that time: lepers. Indeed, shortly before his arrest and execution, where do we find Jesus? In the house of Simon the leper in the village of Bethany just outside of Jerusalem. The event that occurred there, recounted by Mark, is also of significance. Jesus was eating a meal in Simon's house (a most important sign of acceptance and inclusion by Jesus of a hitherto excluded person) when a woman approached and poured a jar of expensive perfume over Jesus. Some of the disciples present were outraged:

> Jesus was in Bethany at the house of Simon, a man who
> had suffered from a dreaded skin-disease. While Jesus
> was eating, a woman came in with an alabaster jar full
> of a very expensive perfume made of pure nard. She
> broke the jar and poured the perfume on Jesus' head.
> Some of the people there became angry and said to one
> another, 'What was the use of wasting the perfume? It
> could have been sold for more than three hundred
> silver coins and the money given to the poor!'
>
> (Mark 14:4-5)

The disciples were in charity mode. They were thinking of
the good that the sale of the perfume could do for the poor.
Jesus was in justice mode. He recognised the totally other-
directedness and selflessness of the woman's action. She was
aware of the isolation and danger that Jesus had put himself
in because of his love for the poor and marginalised and his
opposition to the structures that made them poor and
marginalised. Thus, she prepared him for his death. Jesus
scolds his disciples:

> He went forward a little, and fell on the ground, and
> prayed that, if it were possible, the hour might pass
> away from him. He said, 'Abba, Father, all things are
> possible for you. Please remove this cup from me.
> However, not what I desire, but what you desire.'
>
> (Mark 14:6-8)

At this stage, Jesus clearly understood that his conflict with
the Jewish religious leaders could only lead to one of two
outcomes. Either he could back down and return to a quiet

life in Galilee as a carpenter or he could do justice and face the inevitable consequences. It was not an easy decision, as the natural human frailty of Jesus is revealed in the Garden of Gethsemane.

> He went a little farther on, threw himself on the ground, and prayed that, if possible, he might not have to go through that time of suffering. 'Father,' he prayed, 'my Father! All things are possible to you. Take this cup of suffering away from me. Yet not what I want, but what you want.'
>
> (Mark 14:35-36)

What Jesus did was indeed remarkable and instructive of all justice volunteers. He did the right thing and followed justice and his Father's wishes. It was the same path followed by numerous people in human history, including Steve Biko, Camilo Torres, Helder Camera and Oscar Romero, as well as the many others whose names we do not know. It was also the path followed by Blessed Edmund Rice. It involved saying 'no' to the world the way it is and dreaming a different world, a world based on justice, freedom and, above all else, hope. It is about stepping into the margins and surrendering oneself. It is about going to places such as Mapepe.

Chapter 15

The Widow's Offering and the Generosity of the Poor

Entering Mapepe for the first time

'THIS IS US HERE', said Fr Oswald as he pulled his 4 x 4 off the main Lusaka to Livingstone road. 'Welcome to Mapepe, Aidan.' As we stepped out of the vehicles and walked down the orchid path into Mapepe, moving through the densely packed, chaotically placed clusters of mud dwellings, news of our arrival spread through the village. People came out to look at what was happening, excited children ran in front and behind us and toddlers and babies broke into tears and ran terrified into their mothers' arms. 'You are the first *muzungu* many of these children have seen up close', Fr Oswald explained. The mothers smiled and waved, knowing that we weren't a danger to their children or community. I smiled and waved back wondering what hopes and dreams these people harboured for the future. Did they see us as, literally, 'some great white hope', as yet more of those *bazungu* who all too often descend upon people in the margins, build up a sense of expectation that change may come about and who, also all too often, shamefully disappear leaving another community let down once again by feigned interest and broken promises? Perhaps they had no expectations at all. People whose hopes have been dashed by false dawns in the past – be it by corrupt politicians who arrive with great fanfare and rhetoric (always at election time) and who vanish with equal predictability after the votes have been secured, or simply by people like us, full of idealism but hopelessly naïve and, ultimately, powerless – have learned a harsh lesson: do not hope for change; the disappointment is too painful. Perhaps I was being too cynical and reading too much into their minds. Perhaps they just wanted to know who we were and what we were doing wandering around their village.

Fr Oswald and Cecilia introduced me to the community leaders and other figures of authority in the village. In all my experiences in Africa I have never felt any sense of hostility, resentment or threat towards me, despite my *muzungu* skin and people's often negative experience of some whites who still behave as if they are in some way superior to Africans. It had been quite the opposite. Among the marginalised I found a profoundly touching acceptance and welcome into their community as one loses one's outsider or separate identity and becomes immersed into this new community, this new family. Mr Mulenga outlined the all too apparent community needs and the proposals which the local community had drawn up in order to provide a better life for the people of Mapepe and, 'most important of all', Mr Mulenga informed us, 'a future of hope and freedom from the slavery of poverty for our children'. The selfless prioritising of children by these communities living in abject poverty and facing such multiple difficulties and immense challenges is uplifting and inspiring. The leaders of these marginalised communities do not place themselves or their futures first. Nor do they look for immediate short-term solutions. It is through education that the cycle of poverty and oppression is broken and people like Mr Mulenga recognise that. All of the proposals for Mapepe were centred on the long-term sustainability of a school. We listened attentively as Mr Mulenga rolled out his community's vision for a better future. They knew what they wanted and what they needed. All they required from us was solidarity, mutual affirmation and recognition, love and financial support.

Immersion and religious education lessons

Ask teachers of religious education in post-primary schools in Ireland today what is the greatest challenge they face on a day-to-day basis and quite a number of them might come up with encouraging students to make the connection between the Gospel and contemporary social living. Anne Looney strongly hints at the challenge and difficulty of teaching religious education:

> For the teacher ... the failure of the imaginative and symbolic leap and ensuing hermeneutic dialogue between the religious tradition and the contemporary cultural context, can be frustrating.[64]

Looney certainly makes a point that many teachers of religious education can relate to. You have a class fully engaged in a lesson on social justice, world poverty or the effect of the Celtic Tiger on Irish society, and just when you think you are safe, you collapse interest in the lesson by asking the class, 'Now, how does this discussion relate to the Gospel? What story speaks to you?' This is usually answered by a shrug of the shoulders and a disengagement from the topic. Making the connection between the concrete setting and religion can often be a frustrating and challenging task. Sometimes it seems easier to simply separate the two and teach religion as an independent academic subject, underpinned by 'nice' isolated stories or episodes without any connection with 'real life'.

Perhaps we, as religion teachers, sometimes fail to present the stories of the Gospel as the challenging and revolutionary lessons they in fact are. Perhaps we make the stories 'safe' – and consequently irrelevant to our concrete contemporary social setting – fearful of the radical spirit that infused the teachings and actions of Jesus and how this might lead us beyond stories to action. My immersion experiences and the inspirational people I have met in the margins have helped me to make 'the imaginative and symbolic leap' and to appreciate the relevance of the Gospel to everyday life.

The story of the Widow's Offering
In a revealing passage in the Gospel of Mark (placed immediately before Jesus speaks of the destruction of the Temple and the worship of wealth that underpinned the religious practice associated with the Temple), we are told the simple yet powerful story of the Widow's Offering:

> As Jesus sat near the Temple treasury, he watched the people as they dropped in their money. Many rich men dropped in a lot of money; then a poor widow came and dropped in two little copper coins, worth

about a penny. He called his disciples together and said to them, 'I tell you that this poor widow put more in the offering box than all the others. For the others put in what they had to spare of their riches, but she, poor as she is, put in all she had – she gave all she had to live on.'

(Mark 12:41-44)

It is a story we are all familiar with and I often use it with students in school as a contrast with the story of the Rich Young Man, who had become corrupted by wealth and possessions so that they had become a burden to him, controlling his own life and making it impossible for him to follow Jesus. He did not own his possessions, they owned him. The rich young man had become a pale shadow of what he could, and should, be. He, like many people in the world today, identified with and found himself in the artificial and false needs of wealth and consumerism. Since he accepted these as his needs (indeed, the only possible needs), he was unable to see the necessity and, perhaps, possibility of turning away from wealth towards the new reality of the Kingdom of God offered by Jesus. I tell my students that if the rich young man was living today he might find his 'being' in his apartment or house, his car, Rolex watch, 42" flat-screen television, holiday home, credit rating – and even his wife (but only in the form of a possession or object of beauty). Then, as now, these possessions had replaced being. What we possess, that we are.

'The poor widow', I then suggest to my students, 'is not corrupted by material goods and wealth and so is able to be a true follower. Her gift is more because she gave everything she had, whereas the rich gave out of their excess.' Then some young lad will put his hand up and point out that the poor widow was not corrupted by materialism and wealth simply because she did not have any and that if she did have an abundance of such things, she too might have acted in precisely the same manner as the rich young man did. 'So you are making a virtue out of poverty, then?'

This is what makes teaching both rewarding and challenging. Young people have an incredible ability to get to the essence of any fundamental issue by clarifying and simplifying the arguments. And they have a wisdom that many of us, as adults, should appreciate. Often, I think, we over complicate matters because we are reluctant to accept the consequences. Take the point under discussion: Jesus' teachings on wealth. The teachings themselves are extremely simple and straightforward. Jesus clearly opposes greed, materialism and exploitation. Again and again he condemned riches as a barrier to God. His love for the poor, the oppressed, the marginalised and outsiders was demonstrated when he associated publically (and dangerously) with Levi the tax collector (Mark 2:13-14), the Syro-Phoenican woman (Mark 7:24-30), sinners (Mark 2:15-17), lepers (Luke 17:11-19) and other sick people who, according to Jewish teachings, were outside of God's favour. His anger at the hypocrisy of Temple worship and fearless challenge to the rich and powerful throughout his ministry ought to make us look at our own form of worship and ask whether or not it presents any challenge to the rich and powerful in society today.

It is not the understanding of the teachings of Jesus which presents us with a problem, it is the outworking of these teachings that gives us a *massive* problem. Jesus loved the poor and the marginalised and shunned the rich and powerful. He pointed the way for us to go if we truly wished to follow him and build the Kingdom of God. For the young rabbi from Nazareth, it is simply not good enough for us to 'privatise' our faith and create a safe 'God-slot' of ritual that will exempt us from the command at the end of mass to 'go in peace to love and serve the Lord'. In other words, we are instructed to carry the sacrifice of Jesus, recreated at mass, into our daily lives. It is little wonder we run for cover.

I suppose that as a teacher of religious education, the story of the Widow's Offering should be a relatively safe lesson and one that delivers a strong message: a poor widow gives everything she has right down to her last coin contrasted with the wealthy who, much more publically, make their ostentatious donations. There is surely only one winner here: the poor woman who gave her all. Yet, as demanded by my students above, a deeper and more definitive exegesis is needed here. How does immersion illuminate us on making this fundamental episode in the Gospel of Mark a reality? How does it challenge us to be in that widow's space today? How does it move us from the charity of the wealthy to the justice of the poor widow? Immersion invites us into the margins and, by allowing oneself to be led there, one moves beyond charity and compassion and discovers justice and solidarity. And it is not simply that we *do justice* when we move to the margins; we *find justice* (and generosity, love and solidarity) there among the people who do justice to us. It was while on immersion in the village of Mapepe that I encountered a most remarkable and touching example of solidarity and generosity.

Mary's story

Mary is a pharmacist in Belfast. She had come to Zambia as one of our volunteers with her husband John, a drama teacher who, when he wasn't in the middle of the physical/building action, was entertaining the children of Mapepe as only a drama teacher can. Aine is a nurse and each day she and Mary would set out into the middle of the rural slum of Mapepe with a care worker and dispense whatever little medicines we had. To watch them gently massage the legs of an AIDS victim or tenderly examine a child suffering from any of the host of diseases that afflict the people there made me realise that your very presence, one touch, affirms the human dignity and fundamental value of those who are condemned to live and die in the margins. These most intense of human contacts allow one to enter into a most intimate and sacred space – that very same space that Veronica entered into when she wiped the bloodied face of Christ on his journey to Golgotha (as illustrated in the Sixth Station of the Cross). In the brokenness of the victim one encounters trust, friendship, understanding and, above all else, love.

I was standing in the bar/common space in the hostel that evening. Some of the guys were playing cards, others were starting a bit of a sing-song and I was having a quiet drink and writing in my journal. 'Aidan', a familiar voice behind me called out. I turned around and saw Seamus O'Reilly, one of the Christian Brothers based in Lusaka and one of our main contacts. Before I had time to ask him to sit down or if he wanted something to drink, he asked me if we had a Mary O'Hare in our party. He had received a phone call from Ireland with a message that she was to ring home immediately. It is never good news if someone from Ireland phones the Christian Brothers' house in the missions with a message to call home. I thanked Seamus for coming around and went to see Mary. The look on her face told me that this certainly was not good news. Mary and John went into a dorm and phoned home. John came out to tell us the sad news that Mary's father had passed away. I said that I would go to the airport with the pair of them the next morning. There was no flight out of Lusaka the next day but we could explore trying to get to Johannesburg or Nairobi. At least then we would be on one of the international 'hubs' with a possibility of catching a connection to London and then home. The guys moved out of one of the male dorms to give John and Mary some space to be together. We said a prayer for the repose of her dear father and that Mary and John would get back as soon as possible with her family.

Mary and John said goodbye to the rest of the volunteers the following morning and we set off for the airport to see how Mary and John could get back. We went to the British Airways Office in the airport and were seen by the assistant at the desk, a young African woman called Sylvia. We explained our situation and she listened attentively and sympathetically. Yes, there was a flight to London the next day but it was already full. Perhaps we might consider the Kenyan Airlines flight to Amsterdam (via Nairobi) the next day also and try to connect for London, Belfast or Dublin from there. That flight was also full. Sylvia spent most of the morning on the phone with the British Airways Head Office in Manchester to decouple Mary and John from our group booking in order that she might be able to transfer them onto the manifest for the following day's flight. The Irish Embassy also was in contact with British Airways to try to move the situation towards a successful resolution. Angela Miyanda was also using all of her contacts likewise. In the middle of this, John's mobile rang. It was his insurance company informing him that they might be able to get two seats on the BA Lusaka to London flight for the next day by offering two passengers who may be flexible in their itinerary a financial inducement to postpone their journey for a couple of days. The downside was that this would cost Mary and John several thousand pounds each, which they probably would not be able to claim back from the insurance company on their return. We informed Sylvia of this proposal. She advised us that she would remain working on our behalf all day if necessary and that rest assured Mary and John would be on the plane the next morning. 'You should not worry about how you get back to London tomorrow. That is my job. Please understand that you will be flying home to be with your family tomorrow.'

Several hours were spent sipping coffee, talking about Mary's father and the profound sense of loss that accompanies the death of a loved one, reflecting on the orphanage in Kabwata, the work in Mapepe, the inspirational people we had met over the previous couple of weeks and life experiences in general. Then we were instructed by the PA system to return to the British Airways Office. Sylvia smiled at us like a close friend who we had known for years and told us that she had indeed been successful: John and Mary should arrive the following morning early and identify themselves to the BA supervisor who will then place them on the standby list. 'Do not worry about this arrangement', she assured us, 'you will be the only two on that list and there are two seats reserved for you.' We thanked her and left once again to return early the next morning. Sylvia texted me later that evening to make sure I fully understood the arrangements and that I should give Mary her condolences and prayers.

The next day turned out exactly as that young African woman had stated. I wonder how many of Sylvia's relatives and loved ones have died and marvel at how she put herself beyond the call of duty to ensure that Mary and John – two complete strangers yet two fellow humans in need – got home. Perhaps those in the margins who have experienced such suffering understand and empathise more with others in similar situations than many in the affluent world, which tends to privatise loss. Certainly, in her dealings with us, Sylvia had done justice and reached out to us in our time of need.

Back to Mapepe and Palm Sunday at St Ignatius' Church

The day after Mary and John left was Sunday. We had been invited to share in the community celebration of liturgy in Mapepe. We arrived at the church in the middle of the village in good time. The children's dancing and the choir's singing had already begun. Energy, joy and celebration were tangible. Anyone who has not been to mass in Africa doesn't know what they are missing. Liturgy in Africa is not about duty or simple ritual. It is alive beyond words! It is also definitely not escapist, other worldly or life denying in the way that some fundamentalist evangelical churches in the undeveloped world are.

The growth of this latter movement may be partly explained by the desperation felt by many people in the margins. The promise of personal salvation in the next life would appear to have a very strong attraction, especially for those who are ignored, shunned and abandoned. Many of these churches are of a very distinctive Pentecostal and charismatic nature with a strong emphasis on healing, miracles, signs and wonder. This has led some of the more extreme adherents of this movement to go into the area of superstition, exorcism and witchcraft with horrific and devastating results. In societies ravaged by poverty, HIV/AIDS and despair, this mixture of traditional African beliefs and distinctive evangelical Christianity can be deadly, especially for women and children. Numerous books, documentaries, newspaper articles and other reports and studies provide compelling evidence of the abuse, brutalisation, torture and ritual murder of women and children accused of possession, witchcraft or being responsible for bringing evil spirits (for example, AIDS or crop failure) into a village or community.[65] People in desperation do, indeed, do desperate things.

I was standing outside of St Ignatius' Church in Lusaka after mass on Palm Sunday a couple of years ago. St Ignatius Parish is one of the more affluent parishes and as this had been the 'English Mass' the congregation was certainly different from what one would normally meet in the Misisi slum or Mapepe. People in Africa are in no rush to run off straight after mass is over and their duty is done, not even after the 'English Mass' at St Ignatius'. I noticed a woman standing near the door of the church looking to go in. She stood out from the rest of the people as she was very shabbily dressed, her body was emaciated and her face skeletal and sore-covered from the ravages of AIDS. Others had spotted her trying to enter the church. Three women from the Catholic Women's Association – identifiable by their distinctive sarongs and head-scarves – and a couple of security staff marched over and presented themselves as a human barricade to stop her entry. They then pushed this poor unfortunate woman outside of the church area, whereupon she shuffled off down the road towards whatever slum she had come from.

I was very indignant at this stage and went up to challenge the women from the Catholic Women's Association. After all, we had just come out of Mass on Palm Sunday, the day we celebrate when Jesus brought his followers to Jerusalem to challenge the hypocrisy of the Jewish religious leaders who had surrounded themselves with wealth, power and privilege by excluding the poor and marginalised. And had I not just witnessed the very same thing? 'No, sir, I am sorry but you are wrong', said one of the women. 'She is a Satanist and she is trying to steal some of the elements for their ritual. You see, they need three things: Holy Water and the Eucharist, which she is trying to steal from the church. They think that their ritual will cure all of them of AIDS.' 'And the third element?' I thought to myself. 'They also need a child', a second woman said, speaking softly. It was then that the chilling poster I have seen displayed in every classroom in every school I have been in Africa became real. The poster is of a small, frightened girl-child sitting huddled in a corner. Beside her the message seeks to tell everyone: 'Sex with me doesn't cure AIDS'.[66]

Liturgical celebration at Mapepe: no priest needed

Thank God the community in Mapepe has not adopted the escapism of this form of religion or the sheer madness of those who have lost all hope and reason. Their religious beliefs are of a deeply liberational nature. On Sunday they come together as a community abandoned by the rich and powerful in order to reunite with each other for the coming week's struggle against the impossible odds they are confronted with. It is not simply survival that is their goal. They, with their meagre material wealth, have dreams and hopes – and they hope to transform their world. The community of Mapepe, like so many of those in the margins who have hope, can overcome challenges which we in the affluent West would run a million miles away from. In modern Ireland, like many countries in Europe, we (those of us who are practising Catholics) have talked ourselves into a crisis over priestly and religious vocations. It seems that some in the Church believe that if seminaries and formation houses were full and if nearly every baptised Catholic in Ireland went to Mass every Sunday, the Church and Ireland would be safe. The more important fundamental questions, however, would not be asked: how do we live up to our baptismal vows? Do we really live out the Gospel values that we claim to espouse? What does it mean to be a Catholic in the world today? Do we put justice and the example of Jesus at the centre of our lives? Do we go to Mass on Sunday and then ignore the marginalised, the homeless, the refugee, the alienated young person, the lonely old person, the sick, the disabled and any other person in need for the rest of the week? Does being a Catholic make a difference to us? It certainly does in Mapepe.

It doesn't matter in Mapepe that there is no resident priest. Indeed, there is no resident priest within miles of Mapepe. Once every couple of months a Salesian priest comes to the church in Mapepe to lead the celebration of Mass. It is a special celebration for the people of that community. What do they do during the weeks when the priest cannot come to Mapepe? The community simply come together themselves to recreate the caring Christian community that is the Kingdom of God in Mapepe. It is the Acts of the Apostles and the early Church all over again, and a spiritual awakening for all of us who are invited to journey on this path. How do they do this without a priest? The people of Mapepe have appointed a prayer leader: a lay person who leads the community's liturgy each week. He is called Mr Changa and during the week he makes concrete blocks; on Sunday he inspires the people.

The liturgy follows precisely the Liturgy of the Word for that particular Sunday. The children lead the procession with one of the Ministers of the Word carrying the Bible aloft, as the choir and congregation sing and sway in praise of what is about to happen. Mr Changa, dressed in a simple white robe, greets and blesses the people from the sanctuary and commences the celebration. Readers read the relevant passages from scripture and the people listen attentively as Mr Changa explains to them in Nyanja and to us in English the message of that day's Gospel, which was the Parable of the Mustard Seed. Mr Changa proclaimed that the Kingdom of God is here in Mapepe and growing just like the mustard seed. 'Look around you and see with great joy how our new school building is growing from the very soil in Mapepe. And it is all of us – the people of Mapepe and our Irish brothers and sisters – who are making this kingdom come about.' Never have I heard the Word of God being preached with such passion and clarity. Mr Changa truly is a man inspired by the Holy Spirit.

The Widow's Offering comes alive in Mapepe

When it came to the Prayers of the Faithful, I was invited up to the front of the altar to ask the people to remember in their prayers Mary and John at their time of loss. The people gave a heartfelt response of sadness and loss. Then one of the readers read out a list of those from Mapepe who had died recently or were sick and in need of our prayers. It was a long list for such a small community. The Prayers of Intercession were followed by the Offertory: gifts from the community for those in need. People were giving whatever few kwacha they had to spare. We joined the line and gave what we had, each of us putting into the collection the equivalent of a couple of pounds. For any one of the people of Mapepe this would have been the equivalent of several days' wages. At the end of the liturgy the notices were read out. Each small Christian community in Mapepe was invited to report back on their work and their plans for the future. Information about forthcoming meetings was given out and we were told that last week's collection amounted to 9,500 kwacha – less than €2. It wouldn't have bought two bottles of beer back in the hostel. The chairperson of the Pastoral Council announced that the money had been spent on buying 'two water melons and some other fruit for the poor people of Mapepe'. 'Well, at least the people of Mapepe will get one big collection this week', I thought to myself. 'They'll be able to put that to some good use.'

After the final blessing, we processed outside to continue our celebrations with the people. There was much dancing and singing amid a great sense of togetherness. Even though there had been no consecration or distribution of Eucharist, there was a profound feeling of communion. Out of the corner of my eye I noticed that Mr Mulenga, Mr Changa and some of the other community leaders were discussing something with Cecilia. She beckoned me to join them. Mr Mulenga was standing with all of the collection in his hand and holding it towards me. Cecilia explained that the community was very pleased that such a large amount of money had been raised at the collection and that it was indeed the largest amount of money they had ever received at the liturgy. However, they were saddened to hear of Mary's loss and wanted to give her a gift to help her at this time of sorrow. Therefore, they asked me if it were possible to bring back the collection with me and give it to Mary? Here was a community in dire and abject poverty that had just received what for them was an enormous sum of money thinking about the needs of others. I thanked the leaders very much for their act of total giving and explained to them that Mary would prefer them to use the money to help the poor in the village and would appreciate their prayers all the more. How often do we, like the rich passing the Temple in the Parable of the Widow's Offering, give from our excess, feeling that we are, in some way, doing something noble and remarkable? Do we ever have the courage to follow the example of the widow and, in the words of Mother Teresa of Calcutta, 'Give until it hurts'? Are we brave enough and do we love enough to give totally and selflessly like the people of Mapepe?

Chapter 16

Are they Poor because we are Rich ... and are we Rich because they are Poor?

YOU KNOW WHEN you meet a person who is on fire. Often, volunteers, on returning from immersion, find it difficult to reconnect with the materialist and selfish universe they left when they went to the margins and have now re-entered. Feelings of sorrow and concern about those whom they have left behind, of deeply missing them, of almost wanting to scream in anger about a world that allows such poverty and suffering to exist, and a burning desire to return to those special places where you have left at least a bit of your heart. Colm MacAindreasa, one of Project Zambia's most energetic and dedicated volunteers, expressed his return from his first immersion experience as follows:

> I left Zambia but never really did. I caught a flight from Lusaka on the Saturday morning and by ten o'clock that night I was – physically at least – back in Ireland. I walked around to Cassidy's Bar, from which I had departed a few weeks previous, and met many of my friends who had seen me off and who had been eagerly awaiting my (and our) return. They are all great supporters of the project – from Eugene the owner, Joe

the manager, every single member of the staff and customers as well. They were all interested to hear how we got on. I talked at them like a man possessed who had to unpack every one of his experiences over the time spent in Zambia. It had to be done there, then and at that time or else, it seemed, the recollection would be lost. But this 'unpacking' of memory was not enough. I missed Africa. At that moment I just wanted to jump on a plane and go back.

Such feelings tend to be common among those who have visited the undeveloped world, either as part of a missionary experience or in some other similar capacity. The volunteer who spends time working in the margins with, for example, Trócaire or Concern returns a transformed person. He/she will look at the world – both locally and globally – in a different way.

Perhaps one reason why immersion volunteers desire and seek out each other's company is that each of them knows and understands what the other is talking about in a way that those who have not experienced immersion do not, indeed, cannot. This, of course, is true of many of life's experiences. All life-changing or other deep formative experiences tend to have a somewhat ineffable quality. Sometimes words and the faculty of reason are insufficient. Some things in life are accessed by the heart; they are felt rather than heard.

The bonds forged and relationships made during the immersion experience – between volunteers and host communities alike – are of a degree and quality which we in the West have, perhaps, lost or that is at least limited to relationships of a deeply personal nature – such as those produced within marriage and family. Therefore, when an opportunity came to meet up with immersion volunteers at a seminar in Dublin a couple of years ago, I jumped at it.

'Do they really want to make poverty history?'

The question 'are they poor because we are rich and are we rich because they are poor?' is an interesting one indeed. I first heard it posed at this seminar. All of us in attendance were of the 'been there, done it, can wear the tee shirt' sort of people. We could all tick every box on any immersion examination, for had we not got all of the practical experience and theory anyone would need? So who was this young nun from India to tell us about poverty and what needs to be done? After all, we knew all of that already from our own immersion experiences. Sr Prema Anthony, a Presentation Sister from India, spoke to the gathered audience. I expected her to give a lecture, the basis of which I would have heard before on a number of occasions. Little did I know what she would say.

This slight young woman got to the microphone and introduced herself. She acted as a justice contact with the Presentation Sisters and had formerly been in ministry in Zambia. 'Okay', I thought, 'she may have better credentials than I have, but so what? I mean, we all know what it's like to go to the margins and besides, I'm sure I've read (and therefore know) more about underdevelopment, exploitation and poverty than she has (and knows). What new insights could she give me?' Sr Prema started her talk by asking us to reflect for a moment on the various campaigns that have hit the media such as the 'Make

Poverty History' coalition and to recall events such as the 'Live Aid' concert of 13 July 1985 ('the day', we were told 'when rock and roll changed the world') and the 'Live 8' concert of 2 July 2005 ('the day', we were told 'when rock began the long walk to justice'). We were then urged to think of the many famous people who wear the white wristband bearing the Make Poverty History logo. Prema then asked us to consider whether or not there is a link between poverty and opulence or greed. I smiled smugly to myself. Of course there is. The problem is blindingly simple: poverty is created by greed. While some sections of our world live in opulence and wealth, the vast majority of humankind struggles to survive. And at least one-third of people in the world today – some two billion people – are condemned to live in such abject poverty that they are denied access to clean water, medicine, education and, even, food beyond one simple meal per day, if they are able to get even that. Sr Prema then went on to outline the solution, which is equally blindingly simple and obvious – and challenging.

'Alright', Prema said, 'we all accept that there is a link between richness and poverty. The affluent lifestyle of the rich and powerful necessitates the poverty and disempowerment of those in the margins. How can we change this unjust world ... if we really want to change this world?' She paused for a moment and then, in a quiet and unassuming manner, raised some challenging and probing questions on the Make Poverty History movement. 'Yes, let's make poverty history', she said 'but let's be clear on the implications and means of achieving this.' Sr Prema went on to point out that, if there is a direct causal link between the opulent and obscene wealth in the Western world and the dire crushing poverty in the Third World, then the overcoming of this situation will require a massive redistribution of wealth and resources. 'Perhaps, instead of talking about making poverty history, let's look at making greed and excess wealth history', she suggested. 'If we did that then we would abolish poverty. I wonder how many of the fabulously wealthy celebrities and personalities would agree to give up their riches? Perhaps many of them might look to support a different (and much safer) cause.'

'But do *you* really want to make poverty history?'

Prema certainly brought the house down with that one. Yet, before any of us got too self-congratulatory, the young Indian Sister started to disturb our peace. She urged us to forget about the super rich and, instead, look at our own personal role in issues of justice and poverty. It is all too easy to look at governments, G8/G20, multi-national corporations, the globalisation agenda and the fabulously wealthy and, in so doing, absolve ourselves of all blame and responsibility for the way the world is. We can all too easily fall into the trap of thanking God for not making us like those others! You and I didn't create the injustices of the world, they did. We don't perpetuate poverty and peddle misery on countless millions in the world today, they do. We are innocent, they are guilty – or so we thought.

Sr Prema invited us to consider that almost every action we engage in is a social and, indeed, political action that affects other people. How we live our lives has profound effects on others, be it our friends, families, work colleagues, neighbours or people who we do not know but whose lives are, nevertheless, hugely affected by our actions and choices. Every time we walk into a supermarket and buy a jar of coffee, a banana, a bar of chocolate, an avocado or almost any other commodity on the shelves we are engaged in a moral action. Similarly, when we enter a sports shop and buy a pair of trainers or a replica football shirt, or go to a clothes store to buy a tee shirt or a pair of shoes, we are involved in an action that affects other people. Do we ask ourselves if we are contributing to the plight of landless peasants, promoting sweatshop production and the exploitation of child labour by buying products that are produced in unjust conditions? When we buy a can of certain soft drinks do we question the practices of those particular companies against their workers who attempt to establish basic workers' rights through setting up trade unions? Do we consider that by going to one of the outlets of any multi-national fast food chain we are contributing to the destruction of the environment and indigenous cultures? When we call into a garage to put petrol into our cars do we ignore the shameful actions of the oil industry as it extracts its wealth from the ground, completely disinterested in the people who live there and their human rights, as well as to issues of eco-justice?

In the West, we are great beneficiaries of the wonders of modern medicine. Do we ever question the ethical practice of the pharmaceutical companies of testing new drugs on people in the Third World or on the poorer socio-economic groups in our own society? And within our own society, do we ask questions about the gap between the rich and the poor or the fact that many people are homeless in still affluent Ireland today? Do we consider that people with addictions, the self-harming child who has slipped outside of mainstream education and is now engaged in anti-social delinquent behaviour, prisoners and ex-prisoners now excluded from 'mainstream' society, or immigrants and refugees are in need of help or should they be cast adrift and left to their own resources? And what about the elderly, sick and lonely, as well as those with mental health problems and other marginalised groups and individuals? Are they too not our responsibility? When Jesus was criticised by the Jewish religious leaders for causing an affront and scandal in the eyes of 'respectable society' by associating with tax collectors, 'sinners' and other 'outcasts', he had no hesitation in answering them:

> People who are well do not need a doctor, but only those who are sick. I have not come to call respectable people, but outcasts.
>
> (Mark 2:17)

Are we prepared to radically change our lifestyles in order to help to bring justice to the marginalised – both in the Third World and at home – or do we prefer to point to the rich and wealthy while not doing anything ourselves? Are we like the Rich Young Man who wished to follow Jesus but was not prepared to give up his wealth and affluent lifestyle? Sometimes it's easier and safer to blame others.

Chapter 17

Joinourworld.com: An Invitation to Enter the 'Kingdom'

IMAGINE THIS. You live in the Misisi slum in Lusaka. The city itself is quite flat with very few hills. Misisi is one of the lowest points and is built on swampland. During the rainy season it always gets flooded because water from the higher areas inexorably eventually arrives in Misisi – with nowhere to go. Pit latrines burst open and, with nowhere for the water and sewage to go, you exist/survive in an altogether unhealthy environment. It is not for nothing that Misisi is referred to by Zambians as the 'cholera capital of Zambia'. The internet site Wikipedia has a pretty interesting description of Misisi:

> Misisi Compound is a shanty town, which is located in Lusaka, Zambia. Misisi has been identified as one of the five worst slums in Sub Saharan Africa. Due to a lack of resources there has been poor record keeping, but according to best estimates, there are between 80 and 90,000 people living in the area.
>
> The average life expectancy is around 32 years. HIV and AIDS remains a huge problem in Misisi, as with many areas in Africa. Education into prevention and removal of social stigma is a major aim of the Home

Based Care unit. More than 50 percent of children living there have lost at least one parent to HIV/AIDS. There is also a prevalence of many other diseases in the area. Cholera remains a huge problem, due to a lack of clean water. Malaria is also a major issue during the warmer seasons of the year. Health problems related to poverty, such as malnutrition, create huge problems in the day to day lives of the people.[67]

I guess that we can conclude from this description that Misisi is a severely marginalised community. Being born in Misisi will almost inevitably lead to being condemned to a (short) life of extreme poverty and hardship. Day-to-day survival dominates the thoughts and actions of the vast majority of the population. Dreams of a better life remain just that: dreams. All of this makes the vision, actions and energy of Peter Tembo all the more inspiring as he seeks to free his community from such poverty. It also makes clear the importance of the work carried out by immersion groups both to support the efforts within the host communities and, of at least equal importance, the advocacy work immersion volunteers and groups perform on return.

For many, however, the grinding poverty sucks all hope out of them and grinds them down. Some give up believing that change is possible and spend their time and whatever little money they have in the beer hall drinking whatever version of locally distilled alcohol is available. It puts their problems away for a while and puts them somewhere else – out of Misisi. Some go to the 'Blue Water', giant pools of contaminated water at the bottom end of Misisi, and drink some, knowing that this will end their existence within a couple of days. Others find the whole thing too much and just simply give up and fade away and die.

While this daily struggle for survival is going on in Misisi, the people in the slum can look at the long grey wall of concrete block that runs between Misisi and the Kafue Road, which separates them from the Mercedes-Benz showroom, the shopping malls and everything else that celebrates wealth and separates the 'State of Affluence' from Misisi. There are two worlds indeed. When the people of Misisi and every other slum around Lusaka city centre look skywards towards heaven, they cannot fail to see the multi-storey office block that towers above them. The promised land of the 'States of Affluence' is just there, tantalisingly close, almost within their reach. In reality, it is the headquarters of the mobile phone network Celtel. The top stories of the office block are festooned by a massive banner encouraging people to 'joinourworld.com'. For the people who live in slums such as Misisi, such an invitation must seem to be an escape from all their problems. It also, however, must appear to be – as it is – the stuff of impossible dreams. Most of the people, I suspect, simply glimpse at it as one might look at the moon or the stars. It is not for them. It is beyond their imagination, never mind their grasp. The daily struggle for survival for the people in Misisi and their children is not met by dreaming of joining the affluent world. Those in the margins have much more limited aspirations and dreams: they pray and toil for their 'daily bread'. The 'States of Affluence' is not part of their world. They will not answer the invitation to joinourworld.com.

An invitation to the kingdom
Yet, it was precisely these people – the people in the margins

– whom Jesus invited into the Kingdom of God, the new community of God. In Chapter 14 of the Gospel of Luke, our peace and comfortable attitudes are challenged by Jesus as, once again, he turns conventional social mores – and common decency – on their head. The context and setting in which Jesus presents this teaching on the new community of God are of importance. In the beginning of the chapter we see Jesus in the house of a Pharisee where he heals on the Sabbath. We are told that 'they watched him'. It is in this context that he starts to speak to them. He deals with the principles regarding the Sabbath and doing justice to one's fellow men and women. Observing that many of the guests were choosing the best places at the banquet, Jesus launches into a parable that deals with humility and not seeking to exalt oneself, something that the Pharisees were (and many of us are) good at doing. The story of the Wedding Feast (Luke 14:7-11) might appear to be a lesson of humility and hospitality with a rather stern warning or exhortation at the end: 'For everyone who makes himself great will be humbled, and everyone who humbles himself will be made great' (Luke 14:11). Yet it is much more than a plain and simple moral lesson. The true radical nature of the teaching is only revealed by listening further to Jesus. Jesus turns the normal accepted ways of thinking and acting upside down when he addresses his host:

> When you give a lunch or a dinner, do not invite your friends or your brothers or your relatives or your rich neighbours – for they will invite you back, and in this way you will be paid for what you did. When you give a feast, invite the poor, the crippled, the lame and the blind: and you will be blessed, because they are not able

to pay you back. God will repay you on the day the good
people rise from death.

(Luke 14:12-14)

On hearing this, one of the guests at the table jumps up and
says to Jesus, 'How happy are those who will sit down at the
feast in the Kingdom of God!' (Luke 14:15). To eliminate any
confusion or misunderstanding about who will be at this feast,
Jesus goes on to tell the assembled guests the story of the
Great Feast:

> There was once a man who was giving a great feast to
> which he invited many people. When it was time for the
> feast, he sent his servant to tell the guests, 'Come,
> everything is ready!' But they all began, one after
> another, to make excuses. The first one told the servant,
> 'I have bought a field and must go and look at it; please
> accept my apologies.' Another one said, 'I have bought
> five pairs of oxen and am on my way to try them out;
> please accept my apologies.' And another one said, 'I have
> just got married, and for that reason I cannot come.' The
> servant went back and told this to his master. The master
> was furious and said to his servant, 'Hurry out to the
> streets and alleys of the town, and bring back the poor,
> the crippled, the blind and the lame.' Soon the servant
> said, 'Your order has been carried out, sir, but there is
> still room for more.' So the master said to the servant, 'Go
> to the country roads and lanes and make the people come
> in, so that the house will be full. I tell you all that none
> of those men who were invited will taste my dinner!'

(Luke 14:15-24)

So, is it simply that when the invited guests didn't show up the host decided to invite anyone, including 'the poor, the crippled, the blind and the lame'? I would suggest most definitely not. Throughout this episode in the house of the Pharisee, Jesus is unrelenting. 'The poor, the crippled, the blind and the lame' – in other words, the marginalised who make up the vast majority of the population of the world – are not invited simply to make up the numbers. It is those who are neglected and rejected by 'respectable society' who are, in fact, the new Kingdom of God.

But why is this? Was Jesus suggesting that there was a reward in the after life that would compensate for the suffering in this life? Had Jesus, the firebrand radical teacher who fearlessly challenged all authority – both political and religious – until they had to get rid of him, 'copped out' and become 'otherworldly'? Was he making a virtue out of poverty and marginalisation? Was Jesus idealising the poor and oppressed? To answer 'yes' to these questions is, in my opinion, to completely misunderstand what Jesus was trying to teach, as well as what he was attempting to accomplish: his mission ... our mission. If anything, the Jesus who invites the poor and marginalised into the kingdom in fact reveals the true nature of God – the God who suffers and witnesses with the victims of injustice – the Jesus who suffered and died on the cross is the God who takes on the pain and suffering of his people. Jesus identified with the victims of poverty and injustice precisely because they were victims of poverty and injustice. The great German theologian, Dietrich Bonhoeffer, pointed out that 'our God is a suffering God' and that we are 'summoned to share in God's suffering at the hands of a godless world' (written in Berlin's Tegel Prison in 1944).[68] It is no wonder that the God who is justice – and who became incarnate in Jesus of Nazareth, who was born in a manger, lived God's righteous love as servant of all, died on a cross with forgiveness on his lips and rose to inaugurate a new creation – would seek out and identify with those who were victims of injustice.

In Galatians, Paul tells us to 'bear one another's burdens and so fulfil the law of Christ' (6:2). In other words, it is not enough to feel sorry or even emphasise with people's suffering. We must take on their pain and make it ours. We must identify with the other and become his/her brother so that the injustice they are victims of also becomes an injustice that we recognise, experience and confront. The God revealed by Jesus is a God who shares our pain and bears our anguish. The deep meaning of the cross of Christ is that there is no suffering on earth that is not borne by God. To follow Christ is to conform our lives to the way of self-giving love and sacrifice. True discipleship – 'taking up your cross' – is to allow Christ to move us in a dangerous and radical direction. In so doing, the Church cannot be a group of people who are merely worshippers of Christ; rather, the Church becomes Christ himself, taking form in a community that lives for others, caring for neighbours whoever they are and wherever they live. And should we look far to find a 'cross to bear?' Opportunities to encounter God present themselves everyday, especially when we are fortunate enough to encounter the victims of poverty and injustice, the persecuted and marginalised, the abandoned. When we stop looking at joinourworld.com and look into the eyes of someone in need, then, truly, we will have left the 'States of Affluence' and entered the kingdom. Only then are we truly immersed.

Conclusion:

So Where is Immersion Leading Us?

The Parable of the Goats of Mapepe

A rich man bought a farm. It was a big farm that stretched right down the valley and up the hills as far as the eye could see. The soil was very fertile and a river flowed through his land so that he was able to grow many things. He had access to many markets and towns and cities, so much so that his wealth continued to increase almost beyond his imagination. He diversified and bought some goats which he bred and sold at a considerable profit. Life, indeed, was good for the rich man.

Then, one day, some poor people came and set up their homes between the main road and his farm. The poor people were very poor indeed and could only build houses of mud brick and whatever bits and pieces of shelter they could find. Some houses were made of grass and boards. Some people even used asbestos sheets and pipes from the old sewage and water system, which had been abandoned when the government decided to put in a new water and sewage system because urbanisation had meant that the old system had effectively collapsed. In any case, the company that owned the water and sewage contract rights (and which, in turn, was owned by some globalised corporation in the West) had told the government that the old system had to go. There was no profit in trying to maintain the old system – as if the people in the margins count anyway. This coupled with the potential of selling water to the expanding populations in the urban slums made the upgrading of the water supply inexorable.

When a few people started to build their hovels between the main road and the farm, the rich farmer didn't seem to be too concerned. After all, they didn't encroach on his land and their settlement gave him access to a cheap and ready labour force. You can, indeed, get rich by paying people a dollar a day. However, more and more people came to settle on this piece of land and the rich farmer became concerned. Some of the poor people were desperate enough to steal to make ends meet for themselves and their children. They were tough too. People believed that they didn't care about the law and soon – rightly or wrongly – the settlement developed a reputation that had even spread to the surrounding towns. Many believed that this settlement was becoming a village of thieves and robbers – not the sort of people that you and I would want as neighbours.

The farmer started to worry about his new – and uninvited – neighbours. If they were as bad as people said, they might steal what he had; they might even steal his precious goats. This would not do. So the rich farmer got into his car and drove to the land office in the city. These people had to be moved on. Here, however, the rich farmer hit a problem. Although the people of the village did not have permission to build their homes there, the title deeds of the land were in dispute. The water authorities, the roads commission, various tribal chiefs and a host of other groups and individuals held various claims to the land and its access, so it was rather unclear who actually owned it. Therefore, the government was happy enough for the time being to tolerate settlements of migrants from the rural areas moving to the outskirts of the urban areas to grow, so long as the government didn't have to build social infrastructures such as schools and medical centres or provide clean water.

The farmer didn't like this. He feared for his property, especially for his goats. What would happen if the poor people decide to help themselves to his home, his crops and, God forbid, his precious goats? So the farmer went back to the city and bought fence poles, wire and whatever else was needed to build a barrier to keep such people out. He got his men to construct a strong fence around his property. He looked at it and was content again. No one would be able to get in to steal his property. His goats were safe.

What the people of the village made of all of this no one knows. No one bothered to ask them. After all, they were not real neighbours – at least not the sort of neighbours respectable people would like to live beside. The people of the village continued to work very hard to make life better for their children, their old and sick and other vulnerable groups. Despite the poverty, some in the community never gave up hope that life could improve. Then one day a local priest and four young Africans who had been working with the community leaders arrived with some news. Some white people – *bazungu* – from Ireland wanted to come to work alongside the people of the village. Some of the people of the village didn't want to allow these *bazungu* to come to their village. 'White people come and make many promises. Then they leave and go back to their own countries and we do not hear from them again. White people tell lies.' This was the common objection and fear of some of the people, one based, no doubt, on past experience. Yet the priest and the four young Africans told the people of the village that these white people had worked alongside other marginalised people and did not make false promises. So the people decided that these *bazungu* could come and visit them. Then the people of the village would decide for themselves if these white people told lies.

Within one year, the two groups – Africans and Irish – had become one people and together they built a school for the children, homes for the most vulnerable, established a clean water supply and started income generating programmes, such as a piggery and a chicken run. They even planted a great maize field so that the village would be able to help feed itself. The white people became known as '*bazungu sanama*', which means 'white people who do not tell lies'. One of the young *muzungu* women, Caoimhe, loved them so much that she returned to spend five months with them to write down the story of the old people and their daily struggle to support and care for their orphaned grandchildren. 'How can we be the "voice of the voiceless" if we do not have their full story to tell?' was Caoimhe's motto. During this time, the community leaders told her that there were forty-eight 'grandparent-led families' – families in which the grandparents are the primary providers. Caoimhe wanted to do something about this and so she, along with the four young Africans and the community leaders, established a feeding programme for these most vulnerable families. Caoimhe wrote to all her friends in Ireland for financial support for this project. When people read about the plight of these people and understood the love the grandparents had for their grandchildren, naturally, they responded. So the feeding programme started.

Then, one day, some of the old people came up to Caoimhe. They were happy that their grandchildren were being fed and could go to school, but they did not want simply to receive this as a gift. They wanted to do something in return; they wanted to work for it. So, Caoimhe asked the community leaders for advice. They decided that it would be a good idea if the old people established a small agricultural project, where they could grow vegetables to improve the diet of the children at the school. Everyone in the village was very proud of this new project, especially the old people. Until one day the goats broke through the fence and ate lots of the vegetables. Normally, those in the margins will simply be forced to accept this as yet another experience of injustice. Those whose humanity is denied are scarcely going to protest about their human rights being violated. The rich and powerful have little to fear – or so they think.

When Caoimhe, Cecilia, Osten, Derek and Yvonne arrived at the village the next morning they faced quite an extraordinary scene. It seemed that the whole village – from the oldest to the youngest – had assembled at 'the scene of the crime' and they were definitely not one bit happy. There was anger and noise and shouting and, above all, a sense of injustice. 'If we had broken into his farm and stole his food, he would have come with the police to get payment. Just because we are poor doesn't mean that we are nothing!' said one old woman. All of the others agreed and shouted similar sentiments. 'Let us send a delegation around to him and demand that he repays us for our loss!' There was unanimous agreement, expressed with some enthusiasm. Demand – what on earth was happening in the village? The delegation was proposed and elected and was representative of the community: Mr Mulenga (the Chairperson), Cecilia, two old people and Caoimhe.

'Mula bwanji, muntu'

Perhaps more than any other episode, this story illustrates for me what immersion can do, what it can unlock. Sometimes we can get lost in the details and the material achievements. Western materialist rationalism conditions us to quantify success by quantitative materialist criteria. We look at the buildings, the physical structures and the project that we have helped to create and fail to see the qualitative transformation that immersion brings – to all partners. We are focused on 'doing' rather than 'being'. 'Making a difference' is not about building buildings, it is about building relationships that transform all of us by empowering us. The old people of Mapepe, who were the most disempowered section of the community (with, perhaps, the exception of those such as HIV/AIDS victims) and who had suffered an entire life of powerlessness and injustice, for the first time in their lives stood up against the rich and powerful.

We, from the affluent part of the world, similarly found our empowerment by having our humanity affirmed through becoming immersed, through becoming one with the poor and joining their fight for justice. Indeed, the people of Mapepe no longer regard their Irish brothers and sisters simply as 'the whites who do not tell lies'. Increasingly, as you move around Mapepe, Misisi and the other slums and precious spaces in the margins, you hear the greeting, '*Mula bwanji, muntu*'. The last word – '*muntu*' – is an interesting and important one. I had been aware of the term '*muntu*' for a number of years as that is what Africans call each other. It seemed to me to be nothing other than an African equivalent of *muzungu*, which, to an extent, it is. Africans will refer to each other as '*muntu*' or sometimes as 'African child'. It seemed to me to be (and it is) a Bantu term of solidarity or recognition that suggests 'person' or 'fellow human being'. It does not normally extend to *bazungu*. So when we started to be called *muntu*, I was somewhat taken aback as we are, clearly, *bazungu*.

I mentioned this to Peter Tembo to find out what exactly '*muntu*' meant. He was extremely clear on its definition and usage. It does actually mean 'person' or 'human being' and can be, and often is, used in a limited sense by Africans to refer to one another. However, as Peter explained, in its proper sense – and one that eludes the 'outsider' – the word '*muntu*' means much more than that. In its true sense, '*muntu*' means 'essence of humankind' or 'true being' and refers to one who shares that common humanity, rather like the German '*Gattungswesen*' or 'species-being'. It announces a fundamental equality and identity with the other. It negates that most foreign of questions for the Christian – 'Who is my neighbour?' – by making a neighbour of each person. 'All of us are children of the same God', Peter informed me, 'and because of this, we are all brothers and sisters.'

By explaining the true meaning of this one word, Peter had summarised both the Sermon on the Mount and Paul's First Letter to the Corinthianew love that stands above and beyond any relationship based on legalism, agreed social relationships or norms and any other form of social living. It presupposes a new form of love based on an identity with and for the other and a new human person capable of acting out this love. Jesus' message in the Sermon on the Mount is not one concerning law or social obligation and duty; rather, it is one based on the Gospel and love. It demands a liberation from legalism, from convention and accepted social convention. Immersion, by seeking to live out this radical love of Jesus through encountering and embracing the other in the margins, gives an immanent character to what we often make an eschatological ethic by making justice a goal to be realised in some undetermined future. This is the challenge St Paul set to the early Church in Corinth when he reminds us that 'we are all members of one body ... [and] that the members should have the same care for one another. When one member suffers, all the members suffer with it' (Paul 1 Corinthians 12:12, 26). Through becoming immersed with the people of Misisi and Mapepe, we had all become one body.

Immersion is a truly special place to go to. It is a place that one cannot leave. It is a space in which one comes to recognise the true value of humanity and to encounter the Kingdom of God – indeed, to encounter God Himself. In so doing, we become humanised, whole, redeemed, transformed. It is then that we are able to change the world, to turn the world upside down, to revolve it and turn it the right way up – the way it can be; the way it should be. We can make this inhuman world a beautiful place, a place as beautiful as the kingdom announced by the young rabbi. All we have to do is to be like the people of Mapepe and to help bring about the kingdom of social justice, love and freedom – the kingdom we witness when we encounter God in the margins, when we encounter God in the marginalised, when we encounter God in ourselves.

Notes

1. L. Boff, *Jesus Christ Liberator* (Maryknoll: Orbis Books, 1978), p. 205.
2. BBC News Worldwide, 'Big fall in African Life Expectancy' (15 July 2004).
3. Address by former US president, Dwight D. Eisenhower, 'The Chance for Peace', delivered before the American Society of Newspaper Editors, 16 April 1953.
4. USAF Intelligence Targeting Guide, *Air Force Pamphlet* (1998-02-01), p. 180.
5. A 'graded' road is a dirt or gravel road that has been levelled off by an engineering vehicle with a large blade on the front, commonly referred to as a road grader.
6. It is difficult to get universally accepted descriptors for the areas of cramped, squalid conditions in which people in the Third World live. In Kenya, for example, the people will refer to such areas as Kibera slum or Huruma slum, in South Africa they are generally referred to as 'shanty towns', while in Zambia they are called 'compounds'. Needless to say, they have nothing in common with the gated residential compounds of South Africa and the Middle East in which the more affluent live, secure from those on the outside. In this work, I tend to use 'compound', and 'slum' interchangeably.
7. The word '*bazungu*' is the plural of '*muzungu*', which is widely used in southern and eastern Africa to refer to white people. It should not be regarded as derogatory or insulting.
8. T. More, *Utopia* (Harmondsworth: Penguin, 1965), pp. 128–131.
9. The idea of Jesus as 'Liberator' is the central theme of Boff's Christology. See, for example, Boff (1978), pp. 63–79; 264–295.

10. P. McVerry, *Jesus: Social Revolutionary* (Dublin: Veritas, 2008), p. 71.

11. It is now generally accepted that the prayer was in fact composed by Bishop Ken Untener of Saginaw, drafted for a homily by Cardinal John Dearden in November 1979 for a celebration of departed priests. As a reflection on the anniversary of the martyrdom of Bishop Romero, Bishop Untener included in a reflection book a passage titled 'The Mystery of the Romero Prayer'. See www.xaviermissionaries.org.

12. See, for example, E. Bloch, *The Principle of Hope* (Oxford: Basil Blackwell, 1986).

13. McVerry, pp. 19–20.

14. In J. Gremillion (ed.), *The Gospel of Peace and Justice* (New York: Orbis, 1975), pp. 386–387.

15. Op. cit.

16. McVerry, p. 66.

17. M. Meegan, *All Will be Well* (London: Eye Publications, 2006), p. 11.

18. United Nations Children's Fund (UNICEF), *The State of the World's Children* (New York: UN Publications, 2008). See especially the regional report for Africa.

19. L. Goldmann, *Power and Humanism* (Nottingham: Spokesman, 1974), p. 24.

20. See H. Marcuse's excellent work on the desublimation of human consciousness, *One-Dimensional Man* (London: Routledge, 1961).

21. See G. Ritzer, *The McDonaldization of Society* (Thousand Oaks, CA: Pine Forge Press, 1993).

22. J.W. von Goethe, *Faust* (Harmondsworth: Penguin, 1949), part 1, scene 4.

23. Meegan, p. 24.

24. See, for example, J. Calvin, *Concerning the Eternal Predestination of God* (London: James Clarke and Co., 1961), p. 138.

25. United Nations Development Programme, *Human Development Report* (New York: United Nations Publications, 2006), p. 38.
26. Meegan, pp. 33–34.
27. M. Fleshman, 'AIDS orphans: facing Africa's "silent crisis"' in *Africa Recovery* (Geneva: United Nations, 2001), Vol.15, No. 3, p. 1.
28. Ibid.
29. Congregation of the Christian Brothers, *Constitution* (Rome: Christian Brothers, 1985), p. 12.
30. E. Bredin, *Disturbing the Peace: the Way of Disciples* (Blackrock: Columba, 1985).
31. McVerry, p. 51.
32. This was common belief in Jewish society at the time of Jesus and still is among some Christian denominations today, which are based especially on the Calvinist notion that wealth is a sign of justification and predestination of salvation. See, for example, M. Slattery, *Key Ideas in Sociology* (Cheltenham: Nelson Thomas Ltd., 2003), pp. 63–65.
33. L. Ward, 'You're better off backpacking – VSO warns of the perils of "voluntourism"' in *The Guardian*, 14 August 2007.
34. Ibid.
35. Pope Benedict XVI, *Deus caritas est* (Vatican, 2005), n. 31.
36. Ibid.
37. Ibid.
38. This point was taken up and elaborated upon by the President of the Pontifical Council *Cor Unum*, Cardinal Paul Cordes, in a recent interview with *L'Osservatore Romano* (13 November 2009).
39. On the Allegory of the Cave see Plato, *The Republic*, Book VII, 514a–520a.
40. On the relationship between *The Matrix* and Plato's Allegory of the Cave see W. Irwin, *The Matrix and*

Philosophy: Welcome to the Desert of the Real (Chicago: Open Court Publishing, 2002).

41. On the subject of how modern man in the West finds himself living according to various competing and opposing value systems see A. MacIntyre, *After Virtue* (London: Duckworth, 1985), pp. 4–5.

42. M. Fforde, *Desocialisation: the Crisis of Postmodernity* (Manchester: Gabriel Communications Ltd., 2009).

43. On this concept, see S. Avineri, *The Social and Political Thought of Karl Marx* (Cambridge: University Publications, 1968), pp. 86–88.

44. See especially Pope John Paul II, *Sollicitudo rei socialis* (Vatican, 1987); *Veritatis splendor* (Vatican, 1993); *Evangelium vitae* (Vatican, 1995).

45. Pope John Paul II, *Sollicitudo rei socialis*, p. 40.

46. A. MacIntyre, *Whose Justice? Which Rationality?* (London: Duckworth, 1988), p. 1.

47. *Gemeinschaft* and *Gesellschaft* were introduced by the German sociologist Ferdinand Tönnies to describe what he saw as the two primary levels of social living, the former being the community of unified collectivity of shared values, for example, the family, Church and so on; the latter being the association of self-interested individuals.

48. McVerry, p. 19.

49. Ibid., pp. 22–23.

50. Ibid., pp. 46–56.

51. Ibid., p. 51.

52. UNICEF (2008). See especially the regional reports on Africa, Latin America and Asia-Pacific.

53. On this, see H.S. Klein, *The Atlantic Slave Trade* (Cambridge: Cambridge University Press, 1999).

54. See E. Osma czyk and A. Mango (eds), *Encyclopedia of the United Nations and International Agreements* (London: Taylor and Francis, 2003), Vol. 1: A–F, pp. 363–365.

55. See E. Nicholson, 'Red Light on Human Traffic' in *The Guardian* (1 July 2004).

56. See D. Smolin, 'The Two Faces of Inter-Country Adoption' in *The Seton Hall Law Review* (Newark: Seton Hall, 2005), Vol. 35, pp. 403–493.

57. 'Is Inter-Country Adoption Linked to Trafficking for Exploitation?' in *International Social Services Monthly Review* (Geneva: ISS, November–December 2005).

58. 'Country Reports on Human Rights Practices 2007', released by the Bureau of Democracy, Human Rights and Labor, 11 March 2008.

59. See J.J. Rousseau's 1761 novel, *Julie, ou la nouvelle Héloïse*, and his 1762 work, *Du Contrat Social, Principes du droit politique*.

60. N. Klein, *The Shock Doctrine: the Rise of Disaster Capitalism* (London: Penguin, 2007), p. 15.

61. Ibid.

62. Ibid., pp. 3–8.

63. McVerry, p. 23.

64. A. Looney, 'Teaching Religion to Young People Today' in *From Ideal to Action: the Inner Nature of a Catholic School Today*, J. Matthew Feheney (ed.) (Dublin: Veritas, 1996), p. 72.

65. See J. Schnoebelen, 'Witchcraft Allegations, Refugee Protection and Human Rights: a Review of the Evidence' in *New Issues in Refugee Research* (Geneva: UNHCR, 2009), paper no. 169.

66. See also the BBC News Report, 'Angolan Witchcraft Child Victim' (Wednesday, 13 July 2005).

67. www.wikipedia.org/wiki/Misisi.

68. On the theme of the God who Suffers, See D. Bonhoeffer, *The Cost of Discipleship* (New York: Macmillan, 1960), pp. 97–99.

Select Bibliography

L. Boff, *Jesus Christ Liberator* (Maryknoll: Orbis Books, 1978)

D. Bonhoeffer, *The Cost of Discipleship* (New York: Macmillan, 1960)

E. Bredin, *Disturbing the Peace: the way of disciples* (Blackrock: Columba, 1985)

M. Fforde, *Desocialisation: the Crisis of Postmodernity* (Manchester: Gabriel Communications Ltd., 2009)

J. Gremillion (ed.), *The Gospel of Peace and Justice* (New York: Orbis, 1975)

N. Klein, *The Shock Doctrine: the Rise of Disaster Capitalism* (London: Penguin, 2007)

P. McVerry, *Jesus: Social Revolutionary?* (Dublin: Veritas, 2008)

M. Meegan, *All Will be Well* (London: Eye Publications, 2004)

Pope John Paul II, *Sollicitudo rei socialis* (Vatican, 1987)

Pope John Paul II, *Veritatis splendor* (Vatican, 1993)

Pope John Paul II, *Evangelium vitae* (Vatican, 1995)